"My goal for this book was to take the foods we love—no matter how bad they are for us—and make them healthy and flavorful, something I really want to eat."

—Rocco

also by Rocco DiSpirito

Rocco Gets Real: Cook at Home Every Day

Rocco's Real-Life Recipes: Fast Flavor for Everyday

Rocco's Five Minute Flavor: Fabulous Meals
with 5 Ingredients in 5 Minutes

Rocco's Italian-American

Flavor

NOW
EAT
THIS!

Cook it yourself!

NOW EAT THIS!

150 of America's Favorite Comfort Foods, All Under 350 Calories

ROCCO DISPIRITO

BALLANTINE BOOKS 🏛 NEW YORK

Published in the United States by Ballantine Books,
an imprint of The Random House Publishing Group,
a division of Random House, Inc., New York.

BALLANTINE and colophon are registered trademarks of
Random House, Inc.

All photographs by Kritsada Panichgul

Library of Congress Cataloging-in-Publication Data

DiSpirito, Rocco.
  150 of America's favorite comfort foods, all under 350
calories / Rocco DiSpirito.
    p. cm. — (Now eat this!)
  Includes index.
  ISBN 978-0-345-52090-6 (pbk.)
  1. Low-calorie diet—Recipes. 2. Cookery, American. I. Title.
  RM222.2.D578 2010
  641.5'635—dc22   2009052470

Printed in the United States of America

www.ballantinebooks.com

2 4 6 8 9 7 5 3 1

Book design by Liz Cosgrove

I am grateful to those who started me on the journey toward being healthy: David Hammer, Scott Duke, Nick Amico, and Peter Duggan. Special thanks to Geoffrey O'Leary and Scott Cohen for their patience and support.

And to my fans, especially those on twitter and facebook who support my every endeavor by following, responding, and participating. Without your input this book wouldn't be as rich, as comprehensive, and as much fun to make. This is your book as much as it is mine.

acknowledgments

It would be a crime not to thank the following people for their help with this book: Linda Lisco, Michael Pedicone, David Vigliano, Pam Cannon, Jane von Mehren, Paolo Pepe, Susan Corcoran, Anne Watters, Porscha Burke, Lisa Kingsley, Laura Marzen, Ken Carlson, Kritsada, Markus Klinko, and Indrani; my friends at NBC's *The Biggest Loser*: Jillian Michaels, Bob Harper, Ali Sweeny, and all *The Biggest Loser* contestants I have had a chance to work with and learn from—all real winners . . . and all big losers. Reveille: Howard Owens, Mark Koops, and 3 Ball: JD Roth, Todd Lubin; my friends at Ironman: Tom Guthrie, Blair LaHaye, Zach Rosenow, Lisa Bruno, and Chris Ward. My friends at the Nautica series triathlons. The wonderfully talented and generous Donyale McRae, Bonnie Belknap, Francine Matalon-Degni, Carrie Simon, Ashley Sandberg, and very, very special thanks to Kris Kurek, without whom this book would not be what it is.

CONTENTS

INTRODUCTION

how can i be expected to eat "healthy" if the healthy foods aren't the ones i want to eat?

It's a good question that you've probably asked yourself again and again. For many people, the answer is *surrender*. They make no attempt at all to eat healthfully. The consequence of this type of eating, however, is weight gain and oftentimes heart disease, diabetes, or other health problems, as well as a compromised quality of life, and even premature death.

For others, the answer is *self-denial*. They eat only vegetables, or fish, or soy, or chicken, or restrict their diets to low-fat, low-carb, or high-protein foods. They give up pasta, red meat, pork, cheese, fast food, slow food, pizza, or alcohol. For some it's *desperation*. They take diet pills, vitamins, nutritional supplements, or drugs. They try the Hollywood Diet, the South Beach Diet, the Atkins Diet, the banana diet, the grapefruit diet, or the cabbage diet.

Recent statistics from the Centers for Disease Control and Prevention put the number of overweight or obese Americans at more than 60 percent. We've all heard the stories, read the magazine articles, and watched the talk shows. America is seriously fat and seriously unhealthy. As crazy as it all sounds, you—or someone you know—have probably tried at least one of the aforementioned tactics in an effort to lose weight, get healthy, and look and feel good. I say: Stop the madness.

It's not madness to want to look and feel good—and we should all want to be healthy—but I believe the way we're going about it is colossally wrong. The real answer to that eternal question about eating "healthy" is to eat the foods you like, but eat healthful versions of them. That's what this book is all about.

"bad boys" made good

So why did I write this book? I am not a doctor, nutritionist, or physical trainer. I am a chef. To author most cookbooks, this qualification would be more than enough, as it was for me in writing my previous books. But *Now Eat This!* differs from my prior cookbooks because it's informed by my quest to live a healthier lifestyle. And while I don't make medical claims or offer specific health advice here, I do explore healthful eating within these 150 recipes.

More specifically, I take on America's favorite "bad boys"—those foods that we desperately love but that really aren't good for us. I call them "downfall dishes" because these are the foods that weaken your resolve to the point of breakdown. No matter what diet you're on or how healthy you hope to be, you just can't resist them. For me, it's fried chicken, mac 'n' cheese, and pizza. I am guessing that many of your biggest downfall dishes can also be found in this book.

I used social networking sites to research what Americans considered to be their favorite foods, and from this data I compiled a list of America's top 150 downfall dishes—things like burgers, pizza, pasta, brownies, chocolate chip cookies, and ice cream—which I then set out to reinvent with much less fat, far fewer calories, and zero sugar. My goal wasn't to merely hang on to some sliver of flavor but to bust the code entirely and make over these favorite dishes so that above all, they tasted great—but had a calorie count of 350 or fewer for a main-dish serving and much less fat. In fact, if you look at the traditional fat and calories listed for each dish, you'll see that I was able to reduce the fat by an average of 66 percent and reduce the calories by an average of 83 percent—and still have it taste delicious.

This has not been accomplished by employing the kind of crazy food science that results in yogurt that contains omega-3 fish oils, or peanut butter boosted with antioxidants, but by using real, fresh ingredients—and by swapping high-calorie and high-fat ingredients and cooking methods for far more healthful yet flavorful ones. Nor was it accomplished by making the portion sizes minuscule. The serving sizes here are generous but reasonable. You'll push away from the table feeling thoroughly satisfied and guilt-free.

As a chef, I know how to do one thing: cook food and make it taste great. In this book, I have simply set up parameters taken from personal experience and conventional wisdom that make these formerly high-calorie, high-fat foods taste great in their new skin.

be in control: cook for yourself

This "I-can-have-my-chicken-cordon-bleu-and-eat-it-too" philosophy may sound impossible, but I guarantee it's entirely possible. There is just one catch: You have to *cook it yourself.*

Before you throw up your hands and walk into a McDonalds and order another not-so Happy Meal, consider this: When you cook, you are in control of everything you put into your pan and thus into your body. You decide how many calories and how many fat grams you eat in a given day. You can still eat a version of your favorite foods. But you have to cook it. You have to make the choice to step into the kitchen instead of pulling into the drive-through or turning to highly processed prepared foods because it seems more convenient.

To help make the choice to cook it yourself easier, I've tried to provide 150 of the easiest and tastiest recipes possible—all under 350 calories per serving. With just a few exceptions, these dishes can be prepared in about 30 minutes and call for everyday items found in your local grocery store; none have long lists of ingredients. They also require no special cookware. Most recipes call for only a few pieces of basic equipment, such as a frying pan, saucepan, baking sheet, or mixing bowl.

from foie gras to the finish line

I am something of a latecomer to the diet/weight loss and exercise experience. I became interested in both in my late thirties, and purely by accident. They were two very different paths that eventually crossed.

Back then my idea of a healthy diet was laughable. "Do I *spread* butter on toast instead of *dipping* it in melted butter? Do I cut back on the foie gras—just eat it every other day instead of twice a day, for lunch and an after-service snack?" Chefs are exposed to limitless quantities of the best food in the world, and we love to eat it all. And for a while, that's what I did.

But then my body began to protest. I have had back problems my whole life and realized that without a lot of painkillers or a miracle, I wouldn't be able to stand at the stove anymore—or stand anywhere, period. And when something gets in the way of my cooking, that something has to change.

After visiting a few traditional doctors who told me to "get used to back pain" or "stay off your feet," I realized I needed a different approach. I got the name of a great chiropractor from a trainer I knew, and he not only got me standing straight again but also got me on my feet and running.

One day I walked in for my regular adjustment, and my chiropractor asked if I would participate in a triathlon for charity. Chefs are suckers for anything having to do with charity, so before I could think, I said yes. Then I asked what I had to do. It was a race in which you swim half a mile, bike fifteen miles, and then top it off with a three-mile run. I am fairly fearless (some say reckless), so I immediately agreed. I began to look into triathlons, and before it really sunk in that I would have to swim, bike, and run those distances, I fell in love with the gear (chefs are notorious gear heads).

But when I started training, the other shoe dropped. I could hardly *walk* a mile, much less run one. My 20 percent body fat probably had something to do with that. So I got serious. I got back in touch with a trainer I had worked with a few years earlier, and he told me what I had to do. I started with a focus on cardio and a modified Atkins diet. I gave up alcohol and carbs and ate high-protein foods. I added to that a regimen of double-cardio sessions six days a week. Within six months my weight and body fat percentage was down substantially (the body fat to 12 percent) and I could run a mile or two without calling the paramedics.

In June that year, I competed in my first triathlon. My goal was simply to finish the race without stretchers being involved.

For a starting time, the participants were broken into male/female age groups called "waves." I was in the second wave. The last group was the "Athena" wave—women who were age sixty and older. On the swimming portion of the race, wave after wave passed me like I was treading water—and most swam over me. When the Athena group eclipsed me, I knew I was in trouble. I had a thirty-minute head start on them!

Out of breath but undeterred, I just kept going. When I eventually got out of the water, my legs felt like jelly, but I hopped on the bike and started peddling. I took on the fifteen miles of Connecticut hills with less trouble than the waves of Todd's Pond, but every mile was still a struggle. I finally got to the transition area to get ready for the run. It was a very hot day, and up until this point I'd never really run three miles without stopping more than a couple of times. That day was no exception. Most of the field had

finished the race by the time I even started the run, but I was happy to be in the game at all. I plodded along and eventually finished, dead last. I didn't care. In fact, I was very proud of myself. It was the beginning of my transformation to a healthier person, and I was thrilled.

In the following months, I continued my diet and training and did a few more triathlons, including the Ironman 70.3 in St. Croix. In Ironman 70.3, athletes swim 1.1 miles, ride 56 miles, and then run a half marathon—13.1 miles. It was a pain fest, but ultimately, a whole lot of fun.

My favorite moment came near the end of the race, when I was running behind a man from Austin, Texas. In Ironman triathlons, your age is written on the back of your calf. I was running behind this guy for miles and could not catch him. When I finally got close enough to read his calf, I saw that he was seventy-two. I laughed and cried all at once.

NOW EAT THIS! INTRODUCTION

The Biggest Loser comes calling

Until my first triathlon, I had only toyed with the idea of healthy cooking. Then, as I continued training and doing triathlons, I got a call from the producers of NBC's *The Biggest Loser*. They asked me to appear on the show as a guest chef and cook for the contestants. I was charged with taking the downfall dishes of each of those contestants—the pizza, chocolate chip ice cream, and fried chicken that had helped make them fat in the first place—and making them over so they had zero fat or cholesterol, zero sodium, no sugar, and nothing artificial, not even sugar substitute.

My first thought was "This cannot be done." But I like to rise to a challenge. I started digging in my bag of culinary tricks, thinking creatively about each dish and how I could set aside a learned overreliance on animal fats, sodium, and sugar to bring great flavor to food.

I wound up developing some very good dishes. One contestant, Mark Kruger, told me he used to eat a tub of mint chocolate chip ice cream every night. When he ate my revised version, it brought tears to his eyes. He thought he would never have the taste of mint chocolate chip ice cream on his tongue again.

Thus the seed for this book was planted.

Although *The Biggest Loser* experience inspired some of the recipes in this book, I was not as stringent with the dietary restrictions in these recipes as was required by the show. After all, that is a competition—and you and I just want to get a great-tasting, healthy meal on the table.

creativity from culinary lockdown

Sometimes when the parameters are the toughest, you do your best work. When I first appeared on *The Biggest Loser*, I must admit I chafed at all the rules. It seemed that just about anything that had any bit of flavor was off-limits: no sugar, no salt, no flour, and barely any fat—the list went on and on. Based on these strict guidelines, I was afraid I wouldn't be able to deliver at my usual high level of flavor. After all, I am the "flavor" guy. People expect that I can make anything taste good. For years, I have explored the intricate relationship between flavor and texture in cooking. I extensively studied the four basic flavors—sour, salt, sweet, and bitter—and discovered that the soul of my cooking was about creating interesting and delicious combinations of those four flavors. Even though I found myself out on a limb many times, most diners and critics agreed that flavor was my thing.

It's not easy to make food taste fresh, interesting, and extremely flavorful even when you have no limitations, so imagine my horror when I saw what I was up against on *The Biggest Loser*. The dietary guidelines are fierce: roughly 1,000 calories per day for a 150-pound person.

When I saw the hugely restrictive guidelines, I felt utterly defeated. How was I supposed to make anything taste good? Where's the butter, the honey, the bacon? How can I cook without bacon? Really!

Needless to say, I had to think and cook in a completely different way than I ever had before. People's health and lives were hanging in the balance, and I had to take it seriously. So I started to think about how I could create the mouthwatering flavor combinations and rich textures of my normal cooking and still remain within the assigned parameters.

I realized that two things were going to save me: the use of flavor agents (foods that are rich in taste but not in calories and fat) and the use of specific cooking techniques like grilling, poaching, baking, broiling, faux frying, and sautéing to create intense, satisfying textures and flavors.

Here's what I have come to rely on in the four years since I have been cooking this way.

Rocco's Can't-Live-Without Ingredients

When you cut fat and sugar out of foods, you cut flavor, too. In order for food to taste good, that flavor and texture needs to be replaced, preferably with something that's a good gustatory/dietary bargain—high-flavor, low-calorie.

These are my favorite ingredients for doing just that. Some of them are straight-up ingredients. They are either naturally low in fat and calories (and using just a little bit goes a long way), or they are actually reduced-fat or reduced-calorie products. They are called for frequently in this book. I often list a favorite brand here because I have found it to be superior in taste, texture, and/or flavor when I tested these recipes. The nutritional breakdowns that accompany each recipe are based on the specific brands I suggest. Feel free, however, to use other favorite or available brands, but know that your calorie count may change.

AROMATICS: Scallions, bulb onions, ginger, garlic, and lemongrass all fall into the ingredient group called aromatics. The name says it all. They add flavor and aroma to foods, big time. I can't use them enough.

CAULIFLOWER: This unassuming veggie makes a wonderful replacement for white potatoes. When treated like a potato—as in the German Sweet Potato Salad (page 190) and Better Than Mashed "Potatoes" (page 192)—it tastes great and mirrors the texture of white potatoes remarkably well. To put it in perspective, ½ cup of potatoes contains 67 calories and 15.6 grams of carbohydrates. The same amount of cauliflower contains 14 calories and 2.5 grams of carbohydrates.

The numbers speak for themselves.

CORNSTARCH: When I was a cocky young chef, I used to make fun of chefs who relied on cornstarch to create texture. I thought of it as cheating. Now I know better. Cornstarch helps create body in soups, sauces, dressings, and fillings that would normally require a lot of fat in the form of cream and butter.

DIJON MUSTARD: Although generally high in sodium, true Dijon mustard is a knockout flavor booster. A tablespoon of strong Dijon can blow up a dish (in a good way) like few ingredients can. Dijon mustard is made from ground yellow mustard seeds, vinegar, and white wine. If you don't like spicy

foods per se, this is your flavor detonator.

EGG SUBSTITUTE: I use egg substitute strategically. It's not great in every dish, but when mixed with lots of other ingredients—like peppers and basil and cheese in the frittata—it works out very well. No flavor is sacrificed, but lots of calories are.

EGG WHITES: Wherever a standard breading procedure is called for in this book (as in most of the faux-fried dishes), I use egg whites instead of whole eggs. Going yolkless spares lots of calories, fat, and cholesterol. All you really need is the protein in the egg white to bind the breadcrumbs to the food, so egg whites do the job very well.

EVAPORATED SKIM MILK: It won't whip like heavy cream but it can stand in for heavy cream—especially when combined with a thickener like cornstarch or flour—to create a smooth, rich texture in certain kinds of sauces.

FRESH HERBS: There are few dishes where some chopped fresh chives or brightly flavored parsley isn't a welcome addition. Fresh herbs such as chives, tarragon, cilantro, and flat-leaf parsley reduce the need to add flavor that comes with fat.

FRESH-SQUEEZED LEMON/CITRUS JUICE: Fresh-squeezed only! Acid is a hugely important tool to make food taste good, and the tension between sweet and sour is what makes many of our favorite dishes so flavorful. Think of the lime in pad Thai or the lemon in sole meunière. If you're on a low-sodium diet, a squeeze of lemon or lime juice can make a dish.

GARLIC: Nature's gift to the palate. Few ingredients aromatize a dish the way garlic does. Using fresh garlic is best, and you can find peeled garlic in most supermarkets (stay away from the chopped garlic products in jars—they stink).

GREEK YOGURT: FAGE (pronounced "fah-yeh") is my favorite brand. It's only yogurt and nothing else and has a naturally thick, creamy texture. When there was room to add more calories to a recipe in this book, I used FAGE Total, which is full-fat yogurt (if a recipe simply calls for Greek yogurt, that means the full-fat stuff). Otherwise, I specify 5%, 2%, and nonfat where needed. This yogurt replaces butter in most recipes almost one to one. It has a nice dairy tang to it and enough fat in the full-fat version to replicate the feel of butter. And if you ever want to reduce the calories even further, you can always substitute full-fat with any of the nonfat, 2%, and 5% varieties.

LOW-SODIUM, LOW-FAT CHICKEN BROTH: I have championed the use of canned chicken broth for many years. Realistically, no one has time to make chicken broth for everyday use. Canned chicken broth comes in low-sodium, low-fat, organic versions, which I recommend. Low-fat canned and boxed chicken broth contains about 10 calories per cup.

LOW-SODIUM SOY SAUCE: Soy sauce is made by fermenting soybeans and water into a dark brew with a singular distinct and intense flavor. A little bit of soy sauce goes a long way. If you're on a low-sodium diet, consider using Bragg's Liquid Aminos (no-salt-added Bragg's has about 60 percent the sodium of regular soy sauce).

NONSTICK COOKING SPRAY: Fat is used in cooking for flavor, texture, and release from cooking vessels and utensils. When we use fat to keep food from sticking, we generally use way too much—which is why this spray is genius. All you really need is a very thin film of fat between the ingredient being cooked and the utensil it's being cooked in to provide the lubrication needed to release the food. This product atomizes oil into a mist so that a perfect coating is possible within seconds. A one-second spray of Pam Original and Pam Olive Oil cooking spray contains 7 calories and less than a gram of fat, compared to the 122 calories and almost 14 grams of fat in a tablespoon of oil—and they do about the same amount of work. In particular, Pam Olive Oil Spray is great for misting breaded foods before baking at high heat (rather than frying) to give them a crisp crust.

PARMIGIANO-REGGIANO CHEESE:

Hands down one of the greatest cheeses on the planet, Parmigiano-Reggiano is made with part-skim milk, so the fat content is reasonable from the start. In recipes that call for Parmigiano-Reggiano, I made sure to keep the calorie counts of the other ingredients low to leave room for the real thing. At 8 grams of fat per ounce (and 1 ounce is a hell of a lot of Parmigiano), it's a decent calorie bargain. There is *no* substitute for real Reggiano.

REAL BACON BITS: I am
an unabashed bacon lover. It's simply salt-cured and smoked pork belly, but it's a miracle—the greatest ingredient on the planet. Part of what makes it so fabulous is the fat, but the other part is the sweet/salty/smoky flavor. It enriches anything it comes in contact with. Many of America's favorite dishes have bacon as an ingredient—Cobb salad, spaghetti carbonara, and BLTs (of course) among them. When I began testing recipes for this book, I reluctantly resigned myself to using turkey bacon only. Then I found this product by Hormel called Real Bacon Bits. It's a low-fat alternative to cooking your own bacon. Here are the stats: 3 ounces of Hormel Real Bacon Bits has 30 calories and 1.5 grams of fat. Comparatively, 3 ounces of cooked bacon slices have 458 calories and 35 grams of fat. Bacon is back, baby!

REDUCED-FAT BLUE CHEESE: Wherever the
creamy, tangy taste of blue cheese is called for in a recipe—blue cheese dressing, Cobb salad, dipping sauce for Buffalo chicken fingers—this product easily stands in for the original. Treasure Cove's version is just as delicious as the full-fat stuff—and has half the fat.

REDUCED-FAT CHEDDAR, 50% AND 75%:
Cabot 50% Reduced-Fat Cheddar is a great substitute for full-fat, higher-calorie cheddar. It has half the fat and all of the flavor. The farmer-owned Vermont cheesemaker has won numerous awards, and I can see why. One ounce of Cabot 50% Reduced-Fat Cheddar contains 70 calories and 4.5 grams of fat. The 75% Reduced-Fat Cheddar contains only 60 calories and 2.5 grams of fat. One ounce of regular cheddar contains 114 calories and 9.4 grams of fat.

REDUCED-SUGAR KETCHUP: For calorie
counters, regular ketchup is a non-starter. Because of ingredients like high-fructose corn syrup, ketchup weighs in at 15 calories a tablespoon. Heinz's reduced-sugar variety has 75 percent less sugar and tastes identical. Agave ketchup is also a good alternative to traditional ketchup.

SALSA, FRESH AND JARRED: Salsa is good
stuff—but be sure to check the jarred variety to make sure no sugar or fat has been added. Store-bought *fresh* salsa appears frequently in this book because there are lots of high-quality prepared salsas out there now. This chunky, spicy relish injects a lot of flavor and texture into food without the fat.

▶ **SALT:** Few ingredients are as essential as salt to make food taste good. I enjoy finishing large roasted meats, fish, and poultry with coarse Morton Kosher salt. Sea salt is a nice option for seasoning soups, sauces, and vegetables during cooking. If you're watching your sodium intake, there are a number of good salt substitute products available such as Morton's Salt Substitute (sodium-free) and Morton's Light Salt (50 percent less sodium than table salt), which are both effective for seasoning and finishing a dish.

▶ **SPICES:** Spices are severely underutilized in American cooking. But not here. Intensely flavored spices and seasonings such as cumin, cayenne, curry powder, smoked paprika, and crushed red pepper are used extensively in this book because they really change the complexion of a dish. Hot spices trick your brain (through your mouth) into thinking food is richer and more robust than it is.

▶ **SPROUTED-GRAIN BREAD:** Many of my recipes call for sprouted-grain bread or rolls. This high-fiber, flourless bread made from sprouted grain won't spike your blood sugar the way bread made from processed white flour does. Ezekiel 4:9 brand tastes great and contains no artificial ingredients.

▶ **SUGAR SUBSTITUTES:** After testing a number of sugar substitute options, which oftentimes left a bitter aftertaste, I found calorie-free Truvia and Splenda to taste and work the best in these recipes. One packet of Truvia, which comes from the stevia plant, is equal to about 2 teaspoons of sugar. Splenda is a chemically processed derivative of sugar, also available in a granulated form, which is a good choice for baking. Most of the time Truvia worked best in savory dishes and Splenda worked best in sweeter dishes and desserts. You can use these sugar substitutes interchangeably for most recipes but since Truvia isn't sold in bulk and there is no specific granulated version for baking, you might want to stick with Splenda in recipes such as the Brownies (page 235) and Triple Chocolate Chocolate Chip Cookies (page 236). When I did a side-by-side experiment I found that four packets of Truvia equaled the sweetness of 4 teaspoons of granulated Splenda, or a 2 to 1 ratio, Truvia to Splenda.

▶ **WHOLE-WHEAT PASTA:** Pasta made from refined white flour is no longer an option if you are trying to lose weight, but whole wheat makes for an acceptable substitute that won't cause you to pack on the pounds. The reason whole-wheat and fiber-enriched pastas are okay and white pasta is not is because of the fiber content. With more fiber comes a slower release of the carbohydrates into the bloodstream and, long story short, less weight gain. There are several good whole-wheat pastas out there and if you overcook the pasta (sounds crazy, I know, because you have been forever told to cook pasta al dente) until it's tender, whole-wheat pasta can taste pretty good. Also try some of the other healthy pasta options such as Ronzoni Healthy Harvest whole-grain pastas, quinoa pasta, and shirataki noodles, as well as spaghetti squash.

flavor-saving fat-free cooking techniques

In order to get the most flavor out of the fewest calories, I experimented with a wide range of cooking techniques while developing these recipes. The following are called for most often in the book and produce the best results when it comes to cooking with less fat.

Broiling: This high-heat technique is perfect when the aim is a charred, crispy texture without sautéing or pan frying, and also for heating a pizza stone until it's very hot. Essentially, a broiler is like a grill but requires no charcoal.

Faux frying: I developed this technique specifically for calorie reduction and weight loss, and it is the superstar technique of this book. Without it there would be no onion rings, chicken fingers, or mozzarella sticks in it. I've replaced pan-frying, deep-fat frying, and sautéing with faux frying and the results are astonishing. I start with a slightly modified breading procedure and ingredients: white flour is replaced with 100 percent whole-wheat flour, whole eggs are replaced with whipped egg whites, and breadcrumbs are replaced with whole-wheat panko breadcrumbs. Whatever is being breaded is carefully placed on a baking rack and sprayed with cooking spray, then baked in a very hot oven. The result is a crisp crust that is ridiculously good. You'll never need to deep-fry again.

Flash frying: This is a high-heat frying technique that requires very little time in the oil, so much less fat is absorbed into the food. A case in point is my Flash-Fried Finger-Lickin' Chicken: The chicken is first poached in chicken broth so that it's almost fully cooked, then coated with buttermilk and whole-wheat flour before being flash fried in 2 quarts of grapeseed oil. Only a couple of tablespoons of oil are absorbed by all of the chicken; in deep-fat frying, *cups* of oil are absorbed.

Grilling: Grilling is an inherently low-fat cooking method. I grill all year round. I use an outdoor grill in the summer and a heavy cast-iron grill pan indoors in the winter. Again, high heat is a must when grilling, both for flavor and for the food to easily come off the grill. A 2-second blast of cooking spray just before placing your ingredients on the grill is highly recommended.

High-heat stovetop cooking: In my traditional way of cooking, I would heat up a cooking vessel, then add oil, butter, or bacon fat to it, let the fat get hot, and then add the ingredients. Needless to say, that method is not applied to the kind of cooking in this book. In these recipes, the method is to get the pan very hot—and I mean *very* hot. The pan is then sprayed with cooking spray, followed immediately by the ingredients that are to be cooked. This method spares you countless calories, and in most cases, the results are nearly identical. Where they're not, I've made other adjustments to achieve the same level of deliciousness. When choosing cookware, go for porcelain-coated cast-iron or nonstick-coated cast iron, or heavy stainless steel. Anything else will *not* give you the results you are looking for.

Poaching: Poaching (cooking food in shallow hot liquid) may be the boring cousin of livelier cooking techniques, and I don't call for it often, but sometimes it's the best way to cook without fat. Always poach in flavored liquids such as chicken broth—water doesn't add any flavor to poached foods.

a word about nutrition, sodium, and personal taste

My goal for this book was to take the foods we love, no matter how bad they are for us, and make them low-fat and low-calorie, eliminating as much sugar and "bad" carbs as possible. You will see that there aren't many places where I offer specific amounts of salt—I prefer to leave that up to personal taste and dietary guidelines. While the recipes in this book are great for people fighting heart disease and diabetes—or those who just want to eat great-tasting, healthful food—they are not meant to be a panacea.

Some ingredients contain levels of sodium with which you may not be comfortable, such as Dijon mustard, Parmigiano-Reggiano cheese, salt, tortillas, tortilla chips, cheese, processed or canned meats/fish, bottled sauces (such as soy sauce, teriyaki sauce, hot sauce, etc.), canned or boxed broth (even low-sodium versions can be higher in sodium than desired, try replacing with water or making homemade stock where you control the amount of salt that's added), bread, canned beans, and some canned items. Replace these items with low-sodium options (of which there are many), refrain from adding salt entirely, or simply add what you can personally afford and still stay healthy.

For those of you counting calories, fat, protein, cholesterol, fiber, sodium, and/or carbs, nutritional information has been provided by a board-certified nutritionist for each and every recipe in the book.

You'll also find a comparison of fat and calories for the traditional preparation of a dish versus the *Now Eat This* version. I used various sources, including nutritional details provided by restaurants and online sources (calorieking.com, insidenova.com, and recipezaar.com, among others) to come up with average calorie and fat counts for the traditional recipe comparisons. For example, traditional Fettuccine Alfredo contains an average of 1,220 calories and 75 grams of fat per serving. My version (page 166) contains 336 calories and 10.4 grams of fat per serving. Both taste good, but one won't clog your arteries and lead to tighter jeans.

find your inner chef

Make these recipes your own. Use your sense of taste and your personal dietary goals to determine any changes you'd make to these dishes. All of the recipes have been carefully tested and retested and are wonderful as they are. But if you feel like adding more salt, or using ingredients like honey instead of sugar substitute, or full-fat, all-natural cheese instead of a low-fat cheese, feel free to do so.

Now Eat This reflects my best efforts to come up with an equation that produces great-tasting versions of favorite foods that are dramatically lower in fat and calories than their original incarnations. It's up to you to add or even subtract fat and/or sugar from these recipes, based on your goals.

I have been waiting years to write this book. I sincerely believe that a chef's point of view was exactly what was missing from the plethora of diet cookbooks out there, and I just couldn't accept the notion that in order to be healthy, we had to give up all the foods we truly love. So I did something about it. The rest is up to you.

Now, *go cook!*

APPETIZERS

GOOEY
JALAPEÑO POPPERS

6 jalapeño peppers

½ cup shredded 75% reduced-fat cheddar, such as Cabot

¼ cup reduced-fat whipped cream cheese, such as Weight Watchers

4 scallions (white and green parts), chopped fine

½ cup whole-wheat flour

1½ cups whole-wheat panko breadcrumbs, such as Ian's All-Natural

4 large egg whites

Salt and freshly ground black pepper

Nonstick cooking spray

½ cup fat-free sour cream, such as Breakstone's

At most chain restaurants, just one serving of this very popular appetizer (I love them!) can register between 500 and 1,000 calories, half of which come from fat. The fat content in this version has been reduced from 36 grams per serving to a paltry 5.3 grams per serving. The combination of a reduced-fat cheddar cheese and baking instead of deep-frying is the secret. Jalapeños bake so nicely, I wonder why poppers were ever deep-fried in the first place! Serves 6

1. Preheat the broiler on high. Place a wire baking rack on a foil-lined baking sheet.

2. Cut each jalapeño in half and scrape out the seeds and membranes. Place the jalapeños on the prepared baking sheet and broil until they begin to char slightly and are partially cooked, about 2 minutes. Allow the jalapeños to cool completely.

3. Preheat the oven to 450°F.

4. In a small bowl, mix together the cheddar cheese, cream cheese, and half of the scallions. Using a teaspoon, fill each jalapeño half with the cheese mixture, packing it in tightly.

5. Put the flour in a shallow dish. Put the panko in a small dish. In a medium bowl, whip the egg whites with a whisk until they are extremely foamy but not quite holding peaks.

6. Working in batches, dredge the jalapeños in the flour, shaking off any excess. Add the jalapeños to the egg whites and toss to coat completely, being careful not to let the filling come out. Add the jalapeños, a few pieces at a time, to the panko and coat completely.

7. Spread the jalapeños out on the wire rack and season them generously with salt and pepper. Spray the jalapeños lightly with cooking spray. Bake until the breading is golden brown and crispy and the cheese is melted throughout, about 20 minutes.

8. Meanwhile, in a small bowl, mix together the sour cream and the remaining scallions. Season with salt to taste.

9. Serve the scallion sour cream with the hot poppers.

NOW YOU CAN **EAT THIS!**

	Before	After
Fat	36g	5.3 g
Calories	447	144

Protein: 10 g | Carbohydrates: 16 g
Cholesterol: 14 mg | Fiber: 3 g
Sodium: 239 mg

HOT ARTICHOKE PARMIGIANO DIP

16 thin slices whole-wheat baguette (about ⅙-inch thick)

Salt and freshly ground black pepper

One 14-ounce can quartered artichoke hearts, drained and roughly chopped

3 ounces frozen spinach, thawed and squeezed dry

¾ cup Rocco's Magnificent Mayonnaise (page 200) or store-bought low-fat mayonnaise such as Hellmann's Low-Fat Mayonnaise Dressing

¾ cup grated Parmigiano-Reggiano cheese

2 large garlic cloves, minced

Pinch of crushed red pepper

Although artichokes are delicious, don't try to take down a fresh one. Even chefs have a hard time with them. Instead, use the best quality canned or jarred artichokes you can find. Just stay away from oil-packed artichokes, unless you want to turn this classic dip back into a high-fat dish. Using water-packed artichokes gives us wiggle room to use astonishingly tasty Parmigiano-Reggiano cheese. **Serves 4**

1. Preheat the oven to 450°F. Line a baking sheet with parchment paper.

2. Lay the baguette slices on the prepared baking sheet, and season them to taste with salt and pepper. Bake until the bread slices are golden brown and crisp, turning them once, about 6 minutes.

3. Meanwhile, in a medium bowl, combine the artichoke hearts, spinach, mayonnaise, cheese, garlic, and crushed red pepper. Season with salt and pepper to taste.

4. Remove the baking sheet from the oven (leave the oven on), and set the baguette slices aside.

5. Spread the artichoke mixture in an 8×8-inch baking dish. Bake for 10 minutes.

6. Turn the broiler to high and broil the dip—watching it carefully—until it is golden and bubbly, about 2 minutes. Serve the dip with the toasted baguette slices.

NOW YOU CAN EAT THIS!

	Before	After
Fat	77 g	**9.5 g**
Calories	930	**263**

Protein: 11 g | Carbohydrates: 31 g
Cholesterol: 22 mg | Fiber: 4 g
Sodium: 1,153 mg

CHEDDAR CHEESE FONDUE WITH APPLES AND RADISHES

Cheese fondue is a puddle of warm melted cheese flavored with wine, and I adore it. When it's done right, the cheese coats a piece of fruit or bread with a perfectly satin layer of fatty unctuousness that transforms both parties into something miraculous. Getting that singular texture without all of the fat is a matter of making a thickened wine-shallot reduction and using high-quality low-fat cheddar. I threw in a little bit of bacon because everything's better with it. If you leave it out, though, this reformed fondue contains one tenth the fat of the original. **Serves 4**

1. In a small saucepan, bring the wine, water, and shallot to a boil over high heat. Reduce the heat to low and simmer the mixture until the shallots are tender and about 1 cup of the liquid remains, about 3 minutes.

2. Meanwhile, toss the cheese with the cornstarch in a medium bowl to coat evenly.

3. Whisk a small amount of the cheese mixture into the simmering shallot liquid until it is melted. Continue to whisk in small amounts of the cheese mixture until it is all incorporated and the fondue is smooth and melted. Stir in the bacon and cayenne, and season the fondue with salt and pepper to taste.

4. Transfer the fondue to a fondue pot and serve with the radishes and apples for dipping.

½ cup sweet white wine, such as Riesling

¾ cup water

1 small shallot, minced

8 ounces 50% reduced-fat cheddar cheese, such as Cabot, shredded

1 tablespoon cornstarch

3 tablespoons real bacon bits, such as Hormel Real Bacon Bits

Pinch of cayenne pepper

Salt and freshly ground ground black pepper

1 cup radishes

2 Granny Smith apples, cored and cut into wedges

Healthy Tips

Adding a small amount of cornstarch to a dish that would normally require cream or butter can provide body and creaminess without adding a lick of fat.

NOW YOU CAN **EAT THIS!**

	Before	After
Fat	80g	**10.3 g**
Calories	1,490	**248**

Protein: 19 g | Carbohydrates: 18 g
Cholesterol: 34 mg | Fiber: 3 g
Sodium: 666 mg

BROCCOLI FALAFEL SALAD WITH YOGURT TAHINI DRESSING

1½ cups broccoli florets (cut very small)

Salt

5 garlic cloves

One 14.5-ounce can chickpeas, drained

1 teaspoon ground cumin

Freshly ground black pepper

1 cup whole-wheat panko breadcrumbs, such as Ian's All-Natural

3 large egg whites

½ cup nonfat Greek yogurt

2 tablespoons tahini, such as Sabra

5 cups shredded romaine lettuce

When I lived in Israel I became a huge fan of falafel—a warm pita filled with hot, crispy balls of golden chickpeas, rich sesame dressing, and cool tomatoes. It has so many great flavors—and a lot of fat. This version calls for the falafel to be baked rather than fried—and served as a salad rather than a sandwich. **Serves 4**

1. Preheat the oven to 425°F. Place a wire rack on a foil-lined baking sheet and set it aside.

2. Place the broccoli florets in a medium microwave-safe bowl, season them with salt to taste, and cover the bowl tightly with plastic wrap. Microwave on high, for 2 minutes, or until the florets are tender. Uncover the bowl, transfer the broccoli to a colander, and allow it to cool.

3. While the broccoli is cooling, pulse the garlic in a food processor until it is very finely chopped. Remove 2 cloves' worth of garlic and reserve it in a large bowl.

4. Add the chickpeas and cumin to the food processor, and process until the mixture forms a paste. Scrape the chickpea mixture into a medium bowl and add the broccoli. Season the mixture with salt and pepper to taste, and mix well to combine. Form the falafel into 12 equal balls, and flatten the balls with the palms of your hands to make disks that are slightly less than 1 inch thick.

5. Place the panko in a shallow bowl. In a large bowl, whip the egg whites with a whisk until they are extremely foamy but not quite holding peaks. Working with one at a time, dip the falafel disks into the egg whites and then dredge them in the panko. Place the disks on the wire rack and season them with salt and pepper. Place the baking sheet in the oven and bake until the falafel are golden brown and crispy, about 20 minutes.

6. Meanwhile, add the yogurt and tahini to the bowl containing the reserved garlic. Whisk to make a smooth dressing. Add the romaine to the bowl, season it with salt and pepper, and toss it until it is well coated with the dressing.

7. Divide the salad among 4 plates, top each one with 3 falafel, and serve.

NOW YOU CAN EAT THIS!

	Before	After
Fat	28.7 g	**6 g**
Calories	711	**267**

Protein: 13 g | Carbohydrates: 43 g
Cholesterol: 1 mg | Fiber: 9 g
Sodium: 535 mg

FAUX-FRIED ONION RINGS WITH SMOKY MAYONNAISE

Giving foods that glorious crispy-crunchy texture without a deep fryer isn't easy. The best way to healthfully approximate the deep-fried experience is to use panko breadcrumbs, a mist of cooking spray, and a hot oven. Panko is a Japanese ingredient that used to be found only in Asian supermarkets and health-food stores but is now available everywhere. The crumbs are made from crustless bread, so they're lighter and crunchier than traditional breadcrumbs. **Serves 4**

1. Separate the onions into individual rings. Use only the larger rings for this recipe; reserve the smaller rings for another use. You should have 20 rings total. Lay the rings in a single layer in a large rectangular baking dish. Pour the milk over the rings and allow them to soak for about 20 minutes, turning them once so that all surfaces of the onion rings have been exposed to the milk.

2. Preheat the oven to 425°F. Place a wire baking rack on each of two foil-lined baking sheets, and set them aside.

3. Put the flour in a shallow dish. Put the panko in a small dish. In a large bowl, whip the egg whites with a whisk until they are extremely foamy but not quite holding peaks.

4. Working in batches, remove the onion rings from the milk and dredge them in the flour, shaking off any excess. Add the rings to the egg whites and toss to coat completely. Add the rings, a few pieces at a time, to the panko and coat completely.

5. Spread the onion rings out on the wire racks. Season the rings generously with salt and pepper, and spray them lightly with cooking spray. Bake until the panko is golden brown and crispy and the onions are tender, about 20 minutes.

6. Meanwhile, in a small bowl, whisk together the mayonnaise and the liquid smoke. Season to taste with Tabasco.

7. Serve the onion rings with the mayonnaise for dipping.

4 large Vidalia onions, cut into ½-inch-thick slices

2 cups skim milk

2 cups whole-wheat flour

2 cups whole-wheat panko breadcrumbs, such as Ian's All-Natural

4 large egg whites

Salt and freshly ground black pepper

Nonstick cooking spray

¾ cup Rocco's Magnificent Mayonnaise (page 200) or store-bought reduced-fat mayonnaise such as Hellmann's Low-Fat Mayonnaise Dressing

1 tablespoon liquid smoke, such as Stubb's

Tabasco sauce

NOW YOU CAN **EAT THIS!**

	Before	After
Fat	124g	**4.7 g**
Calories	1,837	**342**

Protein: 14 g | Carbohydrates: 64 g
Cholesterol: 10 mg | Fiber: 8 g
Sodium: 519 mg

STUFFED MUSHROOMS WITH CRABMEAT

4 small portobello mush-
rooms (about 2 ounces each)

Nonstick cooking spray

Salt and freshly ground black
pepper

6 ounces fresh lump
crabmeat

⅓ cup Rocco's Magnificent
Mayonnaise (page 200) or
store-bought low-fat mayonnaise such as Hellmann's
Low-Fat Mayonnaise Dressing

2 tablespoons real bacon bits,
such as Hormel Real Bacon
Bits

¼ cup frozen peas, thawed

3 tablespoons chopped fresh
chives

¼ cup whole-wheat panko
breadcrumbs, such as Ian's
All-Natural

A hollowed-out mushroom cap makes an ideal little edible bowl, perfect for filling with cream cheese and bacon, creamed spinach and
ham, Italian sausage and cheese, or crabmeat. These—made with
fresh crab, a little bit of low-fat mayo, and real bacon—are a real
caloric bargain. A single serving (4 large mushrooms) nets you only
4 grams of fat and just under 120 calories. **Serves 4**

1. Preheat oven to 450°F. Line a baking sheet with foil.

2. Lay the mushrooms on the prepared baking sheet, gill side up.
Spray them with cooking spray, and season with salt and pepper
to taste. Bake until the mushrooms are tender, about 10 minutes.

3. Meanwhile, in a medium bowl, stir together the crabmeat,
mayonnaise, bacon bits, peas, chives, and panko. Season the
mixture with salt and pepper to taste.

4. Divide the mixture among the mushrooms, covering the top of
each mushroom completely and mounding the filling high. Bake
until the crab mixture is hot throughout and beginning to brown,
about 15 minutes. Serve immediately.

NOW YOU CAN **EAT THIS!**

	Before	After
Fat	28g	**2.7 g**
Calories	410	**111**

Protein: 13 g | Carbohydrates: 9 g
Cholesterol: 24 mg | Fiber: 2 g
Sodium: 751 mg

SPICY FRIED CALAMARI WITH LEMON

Fried calamari and tomato sauce is one of the great food combinations. Fried calamari is sweet and crispy, and tomato sauce is slightly acidic—that's a culinary trifecta! Without the fat and calories of the original, you get to eat a lot of this. Use as a spicy fra diavolo pasta sauce as you can handle—the heat will make the dish feel bigger and richer. **Serves 4**

1. Preheat the oven to 450°F. Place a wire rack on a foil-lined baking sheet, and set it aside.

2. Put the flour in a shallow dish. Put the panko in another shallow dish. In a medium bowl, whip the egg whites with a whisk until they are extremely foamy but not quite holding peaks.

3. Working in batches, dredge the calamari in the flour, shaking off any excess. Add the calamari to the egg whites and toss to coat completely. Add the calamari, a few pieces at a time, to the panko to coat completely.

4. Spread the calamari out on the wire rack, and season generously with garlic salt and pepper. Spray the calamari lightly with nonstick cooking spray. Bake until the breading is golden and crispy and the calamari is cooked through, about 14 minutes.

5. Meanwhile, pour the pasta sauce into a small microwave-safe bowl, cover it with plastic wrap, and heat it in the microwave until it is hot, about 2 minutes.

6. Serve the calamari with the lemon wedges and the sauce for dipping.

¾ cup whole-wheat flour

2½ cups whole-wheat panko breadcrumbs, such as Ian's All-Natural

4 large egg whites

8 ounces cleaned calamari bodies, cut into ½-inch-wide rings

Garlic salt

Freshly ground black pepper

Nonstick cooking spray

1 cup fra diavolo pasta sauce, such as Victoria

4 lemon wedges

Healthy Tips

Use my faux-frying technique on any traditionally fried food you can't resist but whose calorie count you can't abide. Try it, veggie tempura style, on thin slices of sweet potato, zucchini, summer squash, carrots, broccoli florets, and mushrooms.

NOW YOU CAN **EAT THIS!**

	Before	After
Fat	81 g	**3.6 g**
Calories	1,180	**208**

Protein: 19 g | Carbohydrates: 27 g
Cholesterol: 132 mg | Fiber: 5 g
Sodium: 155 mg

CRAB CAKES WITH RED PEPPER DRESSING

Most crab cakes are made of breadcrumbs and crab-flavored mayonnaise. And while I agree that mayonnaise is damn good, I just wish it wasn't so fattening. By broiling instead of pan frying, and using low-fat mayo with some green veggies, this very lean version of crab cakes is a new kind of good. **Serves 4**

1. Preheat the broiler on low. Spray a foil-lined baking sheet with cooking spray and set it aside.

2. Place the peas in a small microwave-safe bowl and cover it with plastic wrap. Microwave on high until tender, about 1 minute. Let cool slightly.

3. In a medium bowl, combine the crabmeat, lemon zest and juice, ½ cup of mayonnaise, chives, peas, and panko. Season the crab mixture with salt and pepper to taste, and mix thoroughly. Using your hands, form the mixture into 4 equal cakes.

4. Place the crab cakes on the prepared baking sheet. Broil the crab cakes until they are deep golden brown and hot throughout, about 6 minutes.

5. Meanwhile, combine the pimientos, their liquid, and the remaining mayonnaise in a blender. Puree until smooth. Season with salt and pepper to taste.

6. In a medium bowl, toss the arugula with half of the pimiento dressing. Season the salad with salt and pepper to taste.

7. Serve the crab cakes with the remaining pimiento sauce and the arugula salad.

Healthy Tips

Eat more arugula! If you find yourself with an upset stomach, you might find relief in your salad bowl. Recent research suggests that the peppery green helps reduce the stomach-acid secretion that can irritate gastric ulcers.

Nonstick cooking spray

½ cup frozen peas

9 ounces fresh crabmeat or high-quality canned crabmeat, such as Culinary Reserve

Grated zest of 1 lemon

1 tablespoon fresh lemon juice

½ cup plus 2 tablespoons Rocco's Magnificent Mayonnaise (page 200) or store-bought reduced-fat mayonnaise, such as Hellman's Low-Fat Mayonnaise Dressing

3 tablespoons chopped fresh chives

¼ cup whole-wheat panko breadcrumbs, such as Ian's All-Natural

Salt and freshly ground black pepper

One 4-ounce jar pimientos, with their liquid

4 ounces (about 7 cups) baby arugula

NOW YOU CAN EAT THIS!

	Before	After
Fat	94 g	**4.1 g**
Calories	1,030	**152**

Protein: 16 g | Carbohydrates: 12 g
Cholesterol: 41 mg | Fiber: 2 g
Sodium: 1,096 mg

COCONUT SHRIMP WITH PINEAPPLE PUREE

¼ cup unsweetened large coconut flakes

¾ cup whole-wheat panko breadcrumbs, such as Ian's All-Natural

¼ cup whole-wheat flour

3 egg whites

1 teaspoon coconut extract

8 ounces large shrimp, peeled and deveined

Salt and freshly ground black pepper

One 8-ounce can unsweetened crushed pineapple in juice

½ teaspoon chili garlic sauce, such as Twong Ot Toi Vietnam

At almost 1,200 calories and 33 grams of fat (for an appetizer!), the original version of this favorite starter is incredibly naughty—and, admittedly, incredibly tasty. With apologies to Monty Python, these coconut shrimp have lost their naughty bits but are none the worse for having done so. **Serves 4**

1. Preheat the oven to 350°F. Line a baking sheet with parchment paper.

2. Spread the coconut out on the prepared baking sheet and bake, stirring occasionally, until it is pale golden brown, about 7 minutes. Allow the coconut to cool completely.

3. Place 3 tablespoons of the toasted coconut in the bowl of a food processor, and pulse until it is finely chopped. In a small bowl, combine the pulsed coconut with the panko. (Reserve the remaining 1 tablespoon whole coconut flakes.)

4. Raise the oven temperature to 450°F. Place a wire rack on a baking sheet and set it aside.

5. Place the flour in a shallow dish. In a medium bowl, whip the egg whites with a whisk until they are extremely foamy but not quite holding peaks; whisk the coconut extract into the egg whites. Dredge the shrimp in the flour, shaking off any excess. Add the shrimp to the egg whites and toss to coat completely. Then add the shrimp, a few at a time, to the coconut-panko mixture and coat completely.

6. Place the breaded shrimp on the wire rack and season them generously with salt and pepper. Bake until the breading is golden and crispy and the shrimp are cooked through, about 8 minutes.

7. Meanwhile, in a blender, puree the pineapple (with its juice) with the chili garlic sauce until smooth. Season with salt and pepper to taste.

8. Sprinkle the remaining 1 tablespoon coconut flakes over the shrimp. Serve with the pineapple sauce for dipping.

NOW YOU CAN EAT THIS!

	Before	After
Fat	33.2 g	**3.6 g**
Calories	1,176	**178**

Protein: 13 g | Carbohydrates: 23 g
Cholesterol: 65 mg | Fiber: 3 g
Sodium: 277 mg

OYSTERS ROCKEFELLER

Oysters Rockefeller was created in New Orleans at the turn of the last century. It was named for John D. Rockefeller, the richest man in America at the time, because he and the dish had something in common. If you don't overcook them, oysters are juicy and creamy and taste luxuriously rich. Without changing too much from the classic recipe (aside from reducing the loads of butter), the fat content went from 22 grams to just under 6 grams—with most of that coming from the oysters themselves. This dish is a fabulous throwback that won't set *you* back. Oysters Rockefeller are baked in piles of coarse salt not just to anchor the liquid in the oyster shell but also because salt is an excellent conductor of heat. **Serves 4**

1 tablespoon butter

½ small yellow onion, chopped fine

1 garlic clove, minced

1 dozen oysters on the half shell, liquor reserved from shucking

⅓ cup evaporated skim milk

1½ cups fresh chopped spinach

¼ cup whole-wheat panko breadcrumbs, such as Ian's All-Natural

3 tablespoons grated Parmigiano-Reggiano cheese

Salt and freshly ground black pepper

5 cups coarse (kosher) salt

1. Heat a medium nonstick sauté pan over medium heat. When the pan is hot, add the butter. When butter has melted, add the onion and garlic to the pan. Sauté until the onion is translucent, about 4 minutes.

2. Add about ¼ cup of the oyster liquor, the evaporated milk, and the spinach to the pan. Raise the heat to high and boil the sauce until most of the liquid has evaporated, about 6 minutes. Stir in the panko and 2 tablespoons of the cheese. Season the spinach mixture with salt and pepper to taste. Refrigerate the mixture until cold, about 1 hour.

3. Preheat the oven to 450°F.

4. Spread the coarse salt out in a large shallow baking dish. Lay the oysters in the salt, nestling them in slightly so they are level and secure. Divide the spinach mixture among the oysters, and sprinkle with the remaining 1 tablespoon cheese. Bake until the oysters are golden and bubbling around the edges, 10 to 12 minutes. Serve immediately.

NOW YOU CAN **EAT THIS!**

	Before	After
Fat	22g	**6 g**
Calories	325	**127**

Protein: 8 g | Carbohydrates: 9 g
Cholesterol: 40 mg | Fiber: 1 g
Sodium: 329 mg

TUNA TARTARE WITH GINGER AND SHIITAKE MUSHROOMS

8 ounces sushi-grade tuna

¼ cup Rockin' Asian Stir-Fry Sauce (page 210) or store-bought low-fat, low-calorie Asian sauce

3 scallions (white and green parts), sliced thin on the diagonal

1 tablespoon chopped fresh ginger

Grated zest of 1 lime

3 tablespoons fresh lime juice

6 shiitake mushrooms, stems removed and discarded, caps sliced very thin

1 tablespoon black sesame seeds

Salt and freshly ground black pepper

4 tablespoons textured vegetable protein, such as Bob's Red Mill

I'm a huge fan of raw tuna. The trick is to get high-quality tuna—called "sushi grade." If you don't want to eat raw tuna, you can sear it whole in a hot pan until it's cooked to your liking, then slice and serve it with the sauce and the mushroom salad. Textured vegetable protein can be found in the health-food aisle of most major supermarkets.

Serves 4

1. Cut the tuna into small dice. Put it in a medium bowl and cover with plastic wrap. Chill in the refrigerator until it is very cold, about 30 minutes.

2. When ready to serve, mix the tuna with the Asian sauce, half of the scallions, the ginger, the lime zest, and 1 tablespoon of the lime juice. Taste, and adjust the seasonings if necessary.

3. In the center of each of 4 salad plates, form a mound of tuna. In a small bowl, mix the remaining scallions with the mushrooms, sesame seeds, and remaining 2 tablespoons of lime juice. Season the mushroom salad with salt and pepper to taste.

4. Sprinkle the textured vegetable protein over the tuna, and then pile the mushroom salad on top. Serve immediately.

NOW YOU CAN EAT THIS!

	Before	After
Fat	26 g	2.1 g
Calories	357	128

Protein: 18 g | Carbohydrates: 10 g
Cholesterol: 26 mg | Fiber: 2 g
Sodium: 415 mg

Healthy Tips

Thinking about going vegan? Replace the ground meat in any recipe in this book with textured vegetable protein (TVP), a soy product that has a texture similar to ground meat when cooked. TVP works well in dishes such as casseroles, pasta sauces, vegetarian soups, and chili. It absorbs spices and flavorings well—much like tofu and rice—making it an extremely versatile staple for those who want to eschew (not chew) meat.

SALMON AND UN-FRIED GREEN PEPPER CROQUETTES

Nonstick cooking spray

One 6-ounce can salmon, such as Bumble Bee Prime Fillet Atlantic Salmon, drained

3 ounces fresh salmon fillet, chopped very fine

¼ cup Rocco's Magnificent Mayonnaise (page 200) or store-bought reduced-fat mayonnaise, such as Hellman's Low-Fat Mayonnaise Dressing

⅓ cup jarred fried peppers, such as Cento Sautéed Sweet Peppers with onions, roughly chopped

1 scallion (white and green parts), sliced thin on the diagonal

2 tablespoons chopped fresh flat-leaf parsley

Salt and freshly ground black pepper

½ cup whole-wheat panko breadcrumbs, such as Ian's All-Natural

Everyone loves a good croquette. It almost doesn't matter what's in them—as long as they're filled with something juicy and fried, we like 'em. I think high-quality canned fish such as sardines, tuna, and salmon is underappreciated, so I designed this croquette recipe with canned salmon in mind. To keep it tasting light and fresh, it's mixed with fresh salmon and one of the best jarred foods out there: fried peppers. **Serves 4**

1. Preheat the oven to 450°F. Spray a 12-cup mini-muffin pan with cooking spray, and set it aside.

2. In a medium bowl, combine the canned salmon, fresh salmon, mayonnaise, peppers, scallion, and parsley. Mix the ingredients thoroughly for about 1 minute. (This activates the protein in the raw salmon, which acts as a binder for the mixture.) Season with salt and pepper to taste.

3. Put the panko in a shallow dish. Divide the salmon mixture into 12 equal portions (about 1 ounce each) and roll each portion into a ball. Roll the salmon balls in the panko to coat completely.

4. Place the croquettes into the cups of the prepared muffin pan. Spray the tops of the croquettes with cooking spray. Bake until the breading is golden and they are hot throughout, 8 to 9 minutes.

5. Gently lift the croquettes out of the muffin pan with a fork or a mini offset spatula. Serve immediately.

NOW YOU CAN EAT THIS!

	Before	After
Fat	24.5g	**6 g**
Calories	432	**156**

Protein: 15 g | Carbohydrates: 10 g
Cholesterol: 38 mg | Fiber: 2 g
Sodium: 568 mg

PIGS IN A BLANKET

Along with shrimp puffs and the ubiquitous nut-coated cheese ball, some version of these tasty bits was all the rage at 1950s cocktail parties. They haven't lost their allure—just some fat and calories—in this slimmed-down incarnation that swaps reduced-fat hot dogs and crispy leaves of phyllo for the traditional fat-laden cocktail sausages and crescent-roll dough. **Serves 4**

1. Preheat the oven to 450°F. Line a baking sheet with parchment paper, and set it aside.

2. Lay 1 sheet of phyllo on a work surface (cover the remaining phyllo with a slightly damp kitchen towel to keep it from drying out). Spray the phyllo sheet generously with cooking spray. Top with another sheet of phyllo. Spray the second sheet of phyllo with cooking spray. Cut the phyllo stack lengthwise into 3 strips (each strip should measure about 3×9 inches). Place 1 piece of hot dog at the end of each strip. Fold the sides of the phyllo in to overlap the edges of the hot dog pieces. Roll the hot dogs up tightly to encase them in phyllo. Place the rolled hot dogs, seam side down, on the prepared baking sheet.

3. Repeat the process with the remaining hot dogs and phyllo. When all of the hot-dog packages have been assembled, spray them lightly with cooking spray, and bake until they are golden brown and crispy, about 16 minutes.

4. Meanwhile, bring the milk to a boil in a small nonstick saucepan over high heat. Add the cheese and whisk until it melts. Continue whisking until the sauce is smooth. Whisk in the ketchup and mustard.

5. Serve the hot dogs with the warm sauce for dipping.

8 sheets phyllo dough, thawed if frozen

Nonstick cooking spray

4 reduced-fat hot dogs, such as Ball Park Lite Beef Franks, each cut into 3 pieces

2 tablespoons skim milk

5 slices 2% reduced-fat cheddar singles, roughly chopped

1 tablespoon reduced-sugar ketchup, such as Heinz

2 teaspoons yellow mustard

NOW YOU CAN **EAT THIS!**

	Before	After
Fat	29g	**11.8 g**
Calories	470	**269**

Protein: 14 g | Carbohydrates: 26 g
Cholesterol: 38 mg | Fiber: 1 g
Sodium: 1,357 mg

BUFFALO AND BLUE CHICKEN TENDERS

Buffalo wings are, hands down, one of the greatest dishes ever created. The combo of hot sauce and butter on a crispy chicken wing is sublime. Here's the downside of these tasty things: Wing sauce is high in fat, chicken wings are high in fat, and the accompanying blue cheese dressing is high in fat. It all adds up to an astonishing 1,188 calories per serving. Here, the wings have been replaced with low-fat chicken tenders, the buffalo sauce with a great low-fat store-bought product, and regular blue cheese dressing with reduced-fat blue cheese dressing. **Serves 4**

1. Preheat the oven to 450°F. Place a wire rack on a foil-lined baking sheet, and set it aside.

2. Put the flour in a shallow dish. Put the panko in another shallow dish. In a medium bowl, whip the egg whites with a whisk until they are extremely foamy but not quite holding peaks.

3. Working in batches, dredge the chicken tenders in the flour, shaking off any excess. Add the chicken to the egg whites and toss to coat them completely. Add the chicken, a few pieces at a time, to the bowl of panko and coat completely.

4. Spread the chicken out on the wire rack. Season the chicken well with salt and pepper, and spray it lightly with cooking spray. Bake the tenders until the breading is golden and crispy and the chicken is cooked through, about 14 minutes.

5. Using a pastry brush, brush the chicken fingers with the Buffalo sauce. Arrange the chicken fingers on a platter, and serve with the blue cheese dressing for dipping.

1 cup whole-wheat flour

2½ cups whole-wheat panko breadcrumbs, such as Ian's All-Natural

4 large egg whites

12 ounces chicken tenders

Salt and freshly ground black pepper

Nonstick cooking spray

½ cup Frank's RedHot Buffalo Wings Sauce

½ cup 3-Grams-of-Fat Blue Cheese Dressing (page 201) or store-bought reduced-fat blue cheese dressing, such as Bolthouse Farms

NOW YOU CAN **EAT THIS!**

	Before	After
Fat	132g	**7.5 g**
Calories	1,188	**308**

Protein: 31 g | Carbohydrates: 29 g
Cholesterol: 59 mg | Fiber: 4 g
Sodium: 798 mg

CHICKEN AND RED PEPPER QUESADILLAS

Four 9-inch low-carb tortillas, such as La Tortilla Factory

2 cups shredded 75% reduced-fat cheddar, such as Cabot

2 cups shredded skinless breast meat from a rotisserie or roast chicken

One 8-ounce jar roasted red pepper strips (not oil-packed)

½ cup jarred tomatillo salsa, such as Salpica Cilantro Green Olive Salsa with Roasted Tomatillo

½ cup chopped fresh cilantro

Salt and freshly ground black pepper

Nonstick cooking spray

Using low-carb tortillas was just one of the things I did to improve the health of this cheesy snack. La Tortilla Factory makes a great low-carb tortilla—you really can't tell the difference between it and a traditional tortilla. One other thing you can do to reduce calories is to make sure you remove the skin and any obvious fat from the chicken before shredding it. Serves 4

1. Heat 2 large nonstick sauté pans over medium heat.

2. Lay 2 tortillas on a work surface. Divide the cheddar cheese between the 2 tortillas. Scatter the chicken over the cheese on both tortillas. Divide the red pepper strips, salsa, and cilantro between the tortillas. Season the toppings with salt and pepper to taste. Top each with another tortilla.

3. When the pans are hot, spray them generously with cooking spray. Carefully place 1 quesadilla in each of the pans. Cook until the bottom tortillas are golden and crispy, about 4 minutes.

4. Carefully flip the quesadillas, using a plate if necessary, and continue to cook until the bottom tortillas are golden brown and crispy and the filling is hot throughout, about 4 minutes.

5. Transfer the quesadillas to a cutting board, cut into wedges, and serve immediately.

NOW YOU CAN EAT THIS!

	Before	After
Fat	76g	9.7g
Calories	1,260	299

Protein: 43 g | Carbohydrates: 25 g
Cholesterol: 63 mg | Fiber: 15 g
Sodium: 1,403 mg

LOADED NACHOS WITH TURKEY, BLACK BEANS, AND SALSA

"Loaded" doesn't have to mean loaded with calories. The combination of black beans, salsa, and nonfat Greek yogurt makes this version of nachos a multicultural feast without the fat. Be sure to buy ground turkey made just from turkey breast—not regular ground turkey, which is made from white and dark meat and skin. The fat and caloric content of the two is significantly different. **Serves 4**

1. Preheat the oven to 425°F.

2. Line a baking sheet with foil, and spread the tortilla chips out on the prepared sheet.

3. Heat a large nonstick sauté pan over high heat. When the pan is hot, add the turkey and cook it until it is just cooked through, stirring occasionally, about 5 minutes. Stir the bean dip into the turkey, and season it with salt and pepper to taste.

4. Spoon the turkey mixture over the chips, and sprinkle the cheese on top. Bake for 6 minutes, or until the cheese has melted.

5. Remove the baking sheet from the oven, and top the chips with the salsa. Drop small spoonfuls of the yogurt on top of the nachos (or serve the yogurt on the side if preferred), and scatter the cilantro on top. Serve immediately.

4 ounces baked tortilla chips, such as Baked Tostitos Scoops

8 ounces ground turkey breast

¾ cup fat-free spicy black bean dip, such as Desert Pepper Trading Company

Salt and freshly ground black pepper

1 cup reduced-fat Mexican-style four-cheese blend, such as Weight Watchers

1 cup store-bought fresh salsa

⅔ cup nonfat Greek yogurt

⅔ cup chopped fresh cilantro

NOW YOU CAN EAT THIS!

	Before	After
Fat	51 g	**7 g**
Calories	880	**341**

Protein: 30 g | Carbohydrates: 43 g
Cholesterol: 46 mg | Fiber: 6 g
Sodium: 1,233 mg

BEEF "CARPACCIO" WITH CELERY AND PARMIGIANO-REGGIANO

8 ounces thinly sliced rare roast beef (from the deli counter)

½ cup Rocco's Magnificent Mayonnaise (page 200) or store-bought low-fat mayonnaise such as Hellmann's Low-Fat Mayonnaise Dressing

Gated zest and juice from 1 lemon

3 celery stalks, sliced thin on the diagonal

Salt and freshly ground black pepper

2 ounces (1½ cups) Parmigiano-Reggiano cheese, grated

¼ cup chopped fresh flat-leaf parsley

Paper-thin slices of lean, rare roast beef are healthy on their own, so keeping the toppings light but flavor-packed is the key to the success of this dish. Low-fat mayo amended with lemon juice and zest, crisp celery, and just a little bit of real Parmigiano-Reggiano—grated instead of shaved, for more coverage—does the trick. **Serves 4**

1. Arrange the beef slices on 4 large dinner plates, covering the bottom of each plate completely. Cover the plates with plastic wrap and refrigerate them.

2. To make the dressing, combine the mayonnaise, lemon zest, and lemon juice in a medium bowl. Stir in the sliced celery. Season the dressing with salt and pepper to taste.

3. Remove the chilled plates from the refrigerator. Season the beef generously with salt and pepper. Spoon the dressing evenly over the meat, and then sprinkle the cheese over the dressing. Sprinkle the parsley over the top, and serve immediately.

NOW YOU CAN **EAT THIS!**

	Before	After
Fat	84.1 g	**7.8 g**
Calories	827	**177**

Protein: 17 g | Carbohydrates: 7 g
Cholesterol: 43 mg | Fiber: 1 g
Sodium: 1,037 mg

CRISPY MOZZARELLA STICKS FRA DIAVOLO

½ cup whole-wheat flour

1½ cups whole-wheat panko breadcrumbs, such as Ian's All-Natural

3 large egg whites

8 reduced-fat mozzarella sticks, such as Polly-O 2% Milk Natural Reduced-Fat Mozzarella

Garlic salt

Freshly ground black pepper

Nonstick olive oil cooking spray

1 cup fra diavolo pasta sauce, such as Victoria

Mozzarella sticks may have single-handedly brought down the American health-care system. It's *fried cheese*. Luckily, there are high-quality, reduced-fat mozzarella products available now, and in this recipe there is *no* deep frying. *Fra diavolo* means "brother devil" in Italian; in cooking terms, the phrase refers to fiery food. This favorite snack may be more angelic now, but the sauce is still devilish—in a very good way. **Serves 4**

1. Preheat the oven to 450°F. Place a wire rack on a foil-lined baking sheet, and set it aside.

2. Put the flour in a shallow dish. Put the panko in another shallow dish. In a medium bowl, whip the egg whites with a whisk until they are extremely foamy but not quite holding peaks.

3. Working in batches, dredge the mozzarella sticks in the flour, shaking off any excess. Add the mozzarella sticks to the egg whites and toss to coat completely. Add the mozzarella sticks, a few pieces at a time, to the panko and coat completely.

4. Spread the breaded cheese sticks out on the wire rack. Season them generously with garlic salt and pepper, and spray lightly with cooking spray. Bake until the breading is golden brown and crispy and the cheese is melted throughout, about 15 minutes.

5. Meanwhile, heat the pasta sauce in the microwave or in a small saucepan for 2 minutes, or until it is hot.

6. Serve the mozzarella sticks with the sauce for dipping.

NOW YOU CAN EAT THIS!

	Before	After
Fat	41 g	**7.6 g**
Calories	730	**232**

Protein: 20 g | Carbohydrates: 21 g
Cholesterol: 20 mg | Fiber: 4 g
Sodium: 471 mg

SWEET ONION AND LEEK QUICHE

Because quiche is a custard, by definition it requires that a protein (egg) and fat (cream) mixture set up during baking but remain soft and silky when served at room temperature. Here, the cream has been eliminated completely, making a portion that is just over 200 calories. The flavor comes from caramelized onions, a little bit of bacon, and a small dose of an assertive cheese, such as Gruyère.
Serves 8

1. Preheat the oven to 375°F.

2. Wash the leeks thoroughly to remove any dirt or sand, drain, and dry on paper towels to remove any excess moisture.

3. Heat a large cast-iron skillet over high heat. When the pan is hot, spray it with cooking spray. Add the leeks and onions. Season with salt and pepper to taste. Cover, and cook for 4 minutes, stirring occasionally. Uncover the pan and lower the heat to medium. Continue to cook until the onion mixture is completely soft, about 8 more minutes. Spread the onion mixture on a baking sheet to cool quickly.

4. When the onion mixture is cool, transfer it to a large bowl. Add the bacon, cheese, and egg substitute. Mix until well combined. Season the mixture with salt and pepper, and pour it into the prepared pie shell. Bake the quiche until the filling is set and the crust is golden brown, about 45 minutes.

5. Let the quiche cool slightly. Then cut it into 8 wedges, and serve.

2 medium leeks, cut in half lengthwise and sliced into ⅓-inch-thick half-moons

Nonstick cooking spray

2 medium Vidalia onions, sliced thin

Salt and freshly ground black pepper

6 tablespoons real bacon bits, such as Hormel Real Bacon Bits

1 ounce Gruyère cheese, grated (¼ cup)

1½ cups egg substitute

One 9-inch frozen whole-wheat pie shell, such as Wholly Wholesome, thawed

NOW YOU CAN **EAT THIS!**

	Before	After
Fat	75.1 g	**10.4 g**
Calories	817	**206**

Protein: 11 g | Carbohydrates: 19 g
Cholesterol: 8 mg | Fiber: 3 g
Sodium: 447 mg

PEPPER AND BASIL FRITTATA

Frittata is a dish I have eaten and served for my entire life. It was always there just in case we were hungry or if an unexpected guest dropped by. It's made with fresh eggs and whole vegetables, nothing unhealthy. I never thought of it as unhealthy or fattening. But at 20 grams of fat per portion, its not entirely benign. This dish was a little easier than most to make healthier because it starts out in a good place—but why not have fewer calories without sacrificing flavor?

Serves 6

1 tablespoon extra-virgin olive oil

2 cups cauliflower florets (from ½ head cauliflower)

½ medium zucchini, cut in half lengthwise and sliced into half-moons

2 garlic cloves, minced

Salt and freshly ground black pepper

1 cup jarred roasted red pepper strips (not oil-packed)

¾ cup plus 2 tablespoons grated Parmigiano-Reggiano cheese

½ cup chopped fresh basil

2 cups egg substitute

3 cups romaine lettuce, roughly chopped

1. Preheat the oven to 475°F.

2. Heat an 8-inch nonstick ovenproof sauté pan over medium-high heat. When the pan is hot, add half of the olive oil, then the cauliflower and zucchini. Sauté the vegetables for 5 minutes. Add the garlic, and season the vegetables with salt and pepper to taste. Cover the pan and reduce the heat to low. Continue to cook until the vegetables are tender, another 5 minutes. Add the red pepper strips to the pan and stir to combine. Raise the heat to medium-high.

3. Whisk the ¾ cup cheese, basil, and egg substitute together in a medium bowl. Season the mixture with salt and pepper to taste. With a heat-resistant rubber spatula, stir the egg mixture into the sauté pan. Continue to stir as the eggs begin to solidify. When there are large curds but the mixture is still wet, flatten it slightly with the spatula and stop stirring it. Cook, undisturbed, for 1 minute. Transfer the pan to the oven.

4. Bake the frittata for about 8 minutes or until the eggs are completely set. Remove the pan from the oven and give it a good shake to loosen the frittata. Invert a plate on top of the frittata and flip it over.

5. In a medium bowl, mix the romaine lettuce with the remaining ½ tablespoon olive oil and 2 tablespoons cheese. Season the salad with salt and pepper to taste.

6. Cut the frittata into wedges. Serve hot or at room temperature, with the romaine salad alongside.

NOW YOU CAN **EAT THIS!**

	Before	After
Fat	20.1 g	**5.8 g**
Calories	339	**135**

Protein: 14 g | Carbohydrates: 7 g
Cholesterol: 10 mg | Fiber: 2 g
Sodium: 443 mg

NO-YOLK
DEVILED EGGS

6 large eggs

1 small sweet potato

1 medium shallot, chopped very fine

4 cornichons, chopped fine

1 tablespoon Dijon mustard

1 teaspoon smoked paprika, plus more for dusting

Dash of Tabasco sauce

Salt and freshly ground black pepper

2 tablespoons fresh flat-leaf parsley, chopped fine

The unhealthy parts of deviled eggs are the yolks and the devilish amounts of fat—usually in the form of mayonnaise—that most recipes call for mixing into the yolks. These deviled eggs are yolkless. The traditional seasoned mashed yolks have been replaced with seasoned mashed sweet potatoes mixed with mustard. They look just like the real thing. No one will miss the yolks—or the fat and cholesterol, either. **Serves 6**

1. Place the eggs in a medium saucepan and cover with water by 1 inch. Bring to a full rolling boil over high heat. Then turn the heat down slightly and cook the eggs at a rapid simmer for 5 minutes. Remove the pan from the heat and allow the eggs to sit in the hot water for 8 minutes. Drain the eggs and cover them with ice water. When the eggs have cooled, peel them and cut them in half; discard the yolks.

2. To make the filling, prick the skin of the sweet potato with a fork. Microwave it on high until it is tender, about 6 minutes, turning it once during cooking if you don't have a turntable. When the potato has cooled slightly, cut it in half and scoop the flesh into a medium bowl. Mash the sweet potato with a fork or potato masher until it is smooth. When the sweet potato has cooled completely, stir in the shallot, cornichons, mustard, 1 teaspoon smoked paprika, and Tabasco sauce. Season with salt and pepper to taste.

3. Spoon the sweet potato mixture into a pastry bag. (If you don't have a pastry bag, you can use a resealable plastic bag with one corner snipped off.) Pipe a mound of filling into each egg half. Place the eggs in the refrigerator, covering them very loosely with plastic wrap, and chill until cold.

4. Right before serving, sprinkle the egg halves with the smoked paprika and the parsley.

NOW YOU CAN **EAT THIS!**

	Before	After
Fat	18.6g	**0 g**
Calories	231	**65**

Protein: 4 g | Carbohydrates: 11 g
Cholesterol: 0 mg | Fiber: 1 g
Sodium: 333 mg

"As someone who loves to eat, satisfaction is my main concern. After trying these dishes, I know you'll walk away not only satisfied, but also closer to fitting into your skinny jeans. What could be better?"

SOUPS

FRENCH ONION SOUP

French onion soup began to show up on restaurant menus in the 1960s, when America's interest in French food was piqued by Julia Child. Onions have tremendous nutritional value and have been shown to aid in preventing and treating both cardiovascular disease and certain types of cancer. Though a bowl of French onion soup is full of great things, it also has a fair amount of fat. This recipe calls for reduced-fat Swiss and little to no fat in the general preparation, which trimmed fat and calories by about one-third and one half, respectively. Serves 4

1. Preheat the broiler on high. Line 2 baking sheets with foil. Spray 1 with cooking spray.

2. Separate the onion rings and spread them evenly on the sprayed baking sheet. Spray the rings with cooking spray, and season with salt and pepper to taste. Broil the onions, stirring them occasionally, until they have softened, about 20 minutes.

3. Lay the baguette slices on the other baking sheet, and place it under the broiler. Watching carefully, broil until they are golden brown, about 1 minute per side. Set the baguette toasts aside.

4. Combine the onions, wine, chicken broth, and thyme in a large saucepan. Cover, and bring the liquid to a boil over high heat. Turn the heat to low and simmer gently until the onions are tender, about 15 minutes.

5. Remove the thyme bouquet from the soup, and puree 1 cup of the soup in a blender until smooth. Return the pureed soup to the saucepan. Bring the soup back to a boil; season to taste with salt and pepper.

6. Set 4 ovenproof crocks on a baking sheet. Ladle the soup into the crocks. Top each crock with a baguette toast and 3 slices of cheese. Broil until the cheese is bubbly and golden brown, about 3 minutes.

Nonstick cooking spray

2 large Vidalia onions (about 1½ pounds total), cut into ½-inch-thick slices

Salt and freshly ground black pepper

4 thin slices whole-wheat baguette

½ cup dry white wine

2 cups low-fat, low-sodium chicken broth

3 sprigs fresh thyme, tied in a bouquet with butcher's twine

12 slices reduced-fat Swiss cheese, such as Kraft Deli Fresh

NOW YOU CAN EAT THIS!

	Before	After
Fat	39g	12.9 g
Calories	547	306

Protein: 25 g | Carbohydrates: 24 g
Cholesterol: 30 mg | Fiber: 2 g
Sodium: 599 mg

NEW ENGLAND CLAM CHOWDER

1 medium yellow onion, diced

4 garlic cloves, chopped fine

4 cups cauliflower florets

1½ cups skim milk

Three 6.5-ounce cans chopped clams, with their liquid

2 tablespoons cornstarch

6 tablespoons real bacon bits, such as Hormel Real Bacon Bits

⅔ cup Greek yogurt

2 tablespoons chopped fresh chives

Salt and freshly ground black pepper

This clam chowder has been an American classic since the early 1800s, and it's easy to see why. Cream—strike one! White potatoes—strike two! Bacon—should be strike three, you're out! Here's the good news: By replacing whole milk and cream with skim milk and yogurt, I had a calorie deficit—which I used to include some bacon. Serves 4

1. In a large Dutch oven, combine the onion, garlic, cauliflower, and milk. Bring the mixture to a boil over high heat. Reduce the heat to low, cover, and simmer until the vegetables are tender, about 7 minutes.

2. Strain the clams, reserving the juice. In a medium bowl, whisk the clam juice into the cornstarch.

3. Raise the heat under the Dutch oven to medium, and whisk the cornstarch mixture into the soup. Bring the soup to a boil, whisking constantly. Then reduce the heat and simmer until the soup has thickened, about 2 minutes.

4. Add the clams and bacon to the soup, and remove from the heat. Whisk in the yogurt and chives. Season the soup with salt and pepper to taste, and serve.

NOW YOU CAN EAT THIS!

	Before	After
Fat	33g	**9.1 g**
Calories	480	**299**

Protein: 34 g | Carbohydrates: 24 g
Cholesterol: 121 mg | Fiber: 3 g
Sodium: 1,130 mg

LOBSTER BISQUE

Blush-colored lobster bisque made from flavorful lobster stock has historically suggested the height of elegance. Save this recipe for a leisurely weekend. **Serves 4**

1. Heat a Dutch oven over medium-high heat.

2. While the Dutch oven is heating, break down the lobsters: Remove the claws and place them in a bowl. Twist the heads off the tails. Add the tails to the bowl, and refrigerate. Pull the outer shell of the head off each body; discard the outer shells. Remove and discard the lung sacs, leaving the tomalley (the soft green paste). Finely chop the bodies with a cleaver.

3. When the Dutch oven is hot, spray it with cooking spray. Add the chopped lobster and cook, stirring occasionally, until most of the moisture has evaporated, about 4 minutes. Add the onions, garlic, and paprika and cook, stirring occasionally, until the onions and garlic are fragrant, about 2 minutes. (It is important not to burn the bottom of the pot, so if mixture begins to brown, reduce the heat.)

4. Add the wine and cook until it has reduced by about one-third, about 3 minutes. Add the tomatoes and their juice. Reduce slightly, about 2 minutes. Add the chicken broth and 1¾ cups of the milk; bring to a boil. Reduce the heat to medium-low and cook at a steady simmer, uncovered, for 20 minutes; the liquid should reduce by about half. Let the stock cool for a few minutes.

5. While the stock is simmering, remove the claw and tail lobster meat from the shells, working on a rimmed baking sheet to reserve any juice. Add the juice to the simmering stock. Roughly chop the lobster meat (there should be about 1¼ cups), and set it aside.

6. Pour half of the slightly cooled stock into a blender. Blend with the shells (yes, the shells!) carefully on the lowest speed until it is as smooth as possible. Strain all of the stock through a fine-mesh strainer into a medium saucepan, pressing on the solids to

(continued on next page)

Two 1- to 1¼-pound lobsters, steamed by your fishmonger

Butter-flavored nonstick cooking spray, such as Pam

2 medium onions, cut into medium dice

3 garlic cloves, roughly chopped

1½ teaspoons sweet paprika

½ cup sweet white wine, such as Riesling

One 14.5-ounce can diced tomatoes in juice

1¾ cups low-fat, low-sodium chicken broth

2¼ cups skim milk

1 tablespoon cornstarch

Juice of ½ lemon

Few dashes of Tabasco sauce

Salt and freshly ground black pepper

3 tablespoons chopped fresh chives

NOW YOU CAN EAT THIS!

	Before	After
Fat	26.7 g	**1 g**
Calories	739	**181**

Protein: 17 g | Carbohydrates: 22 g
Cholesterol: 50 mg | Fiber: 3 g
Sodium: 813 mg

extract as much liquid as possible (you should have about 3 cups). Return the pureed stock back to the pot with the remaining stock. Put the pan over high heat and bring to a boil.

7. Meanwhile, whisk the remaining ½ cup milk into the cornstarch in a small bowl. Whisk the cornstarch mixture into the boiling stock. Return to a boil, whisking constantly. Cook until the stock thickens, about 1 minute.

8. Stir in the reserved lobster meat, and remove from the heat. (The residual heat from the soup will warm the lobster meat.) Season the bisque with the lemon juice, Tabasco, and salt and pepper to taste. Stir in the chives, and serve immediately.

CORN CHOWDER

Make this delicious soup in the summer, when you can use corn that was picked that morning. Corn is loaded with sugars and carbs, but that's why we like it so much. I incorporated cauliflower in this soup to reduce the carb count and to add body, without adding the starch and calories of potatoes. Serves 4

1. Heat a Dutch oven over medium heat. When the pot is hot, spray it with cooking spray. Add the onion and corn. Season with salt and pepper to taste. Sauté, stirring occasionally, for 6 minutes, or until the vegetables have started to soften. Add the cauliflower and milk, cover, and bring the soup to a boil. Reduce the heat to medium-low. Simmer the soup until the corn and cauliflower are tender, about 20 minutes.

2. Strain 1 cup of the soup through a sieve. Reserve the solids, and return the liquid to the pot. Pour the contents of the pot into a blender and puree until smooth. Return the soup to the pot, add the strained solids, and bring to a boil.

3. Remove the soup from the heat; stir in the yogurt and scallions. Season with salt and pepper to taste, and serve.

Nonstick cooking spray

1 small yellow onion, cut into small dice

Kernels from 3 ears fresh corn

Salt and freshly ground black pepper

1½ cups cauliflower florets

2½ cups skim milk

One 7-ounce container Greek yogurt

½ bunch scallions (green part only), sliced thin on the diagonal

NOW YOU CAN **EAT THIS!**

	Before	After
Fat	23g	**5.8 g**
Calories	359	**190**

Protein: 10 g | Carbohydrates: 28 g
Cholesterol: 16 mg | Fiber: 3 g
Sodium: 264 mg

BLACK BEAN SOUP

One 14.5-ounce can black beans, with liquid

⅔ cup low-fat, low-sodium chicken broth

⅔ cup store-bought fresh salsa, such as Top Crop

2 teaspoons chili powder

2 tablespoons reduced-sugar ketchup, such as Heinz

3 tablespoons real bacon bits, such as Hormel Real Bacon Bits

Salt and freshly ground black pepper

¼ cup shredded 75% reduced-fat cheddar cheese, such as Cabot

¼ cup nonfat Greek yogurt

⅓ cup chopped fresh cilantro

Black beans are a very good source of cholesterol-lowering fiber and have many healthy properties that make them a good go-to ingredient. The best thing about black beans is their rich, meaty flavor. They lend themselves to many preparations, are great hot or cold, and the best news is that you don't ever have to cook them if you don't have the time or inclination. When purchasing, watch out for sodium levels, and buy organic if you can. Serves 4

1. In a blender, combine half of the beans and all their liquid, the chicken broth, and ⅓ cup of the salsa. Puree the mixture until smooth.

2. Pour the contents of the blender into a medium saucepan and place it over high heat. Add the remaining beans, remaining salsa, chili powder, ketchup, and bacon. Bring the soup to a boil. Then reduce the heat to low. Cook the soup, stirring frequently, until thickened, about 9 minutes. Season with salt and pepper to taste.

3. Ladle the soup into 4 bowls. Top each bowl with cheddar cheese, a dollop of yogurt, and a sprinkling of cilantro, and serve.

NOW YOU CAN EAT THIS!

	Before	After
Fat	7.9 g	2.1 g
Calories	392	129

Protein: 12 g | Carbohydrates: 21 g
Cholesterol: 7 mg | Fiber: 5 g
Sodium: 1,159 mg

TORTILLA SOUP WITH AVOCADO AND CILANTRO

I must admit that I didn't realize at first that tortilla soup was an American favorite, but it slowly dawned on me. One of my favorite hotels serves it, there is a movie called *Tortilla Soup,* and when I asked my Twitter peeps about soups, it came up over and over. Its origins are Mexican, but it has become Americanized over the years. In Mexico City, this soup is made simply with roasted tomatoes, chiles, chicken broth, and corn tortillas. This version is true to the original, with a few additions. **Serves 4**

1. Preheat the oven to 375°F. Line a baking sheet with parchment paper.

2. Cut the tortillas into ¼-inch-wide strips. Place the strips in a single layer on the prepared baking sheet, and bake until golden and crisp, about 9 minutes.

3. Meanwhile, combine the chicken broth, tomatoes, chipotle chiles, salsa, and corn in a medium saucepan. Bring the soup to a boil over high heat. Turn the heat to medium-low and simmer for 8 minutes. Stir the chicken into the soup, and season with salt and pepper to taste.

4. Ladle the soup into 4 bowls. Top each bowl with avocado slices, chopped cilantro, and tortilla strips, and serve.

1 ½ sprouted-corn tortillas, such as Food for Life

⅔ cup low-fat, low-sodium chicken broth

1 cup diced fire-roasted tomatoes, such as Hunt's

2 chipotle chiles in adobo sauce, chopped fine

⅔ cup store-bought hot fresh salsa, such as Santa Barbara

½ cup fresh or frozen corn kernels

1 cup shredded skinless breast meat from a rotisserie or roast chicken

Salt and freshly ground black pepper

⅓ ripe Hass avocado, sliced

⅓ cup chopped fresh cilantro

Healthy Tips

Eat more chiles! The fire in fresh jalapeños and cayenne pepper alike comes from a substance called capsaicin. The more capsaicin in a pepper, the hotter it is. Research has shown that capsaicin lowers cholesterol and triglycerides in the blood, as well as (counterintuitively) protecting against stomach ulcers. It has also been shown to increase metabolism for about 20 minutes after consumption. More flavor, more calories burned. That's a no-brainer.

NOW YOU CAN **EAT THIS!**

	Before	After
Fat	20g	**3.1 g**
Calories	510	**142**

Protein: 12 g | Carbohydrates: 20 g
Cholesterol: 22 mg | Fiber: 3 g
Sodium: 706 mg

CHEDDAR CHEESE AND "POTATO" SOUP

Nonstick cooking spray

2 garlic cloves, minced

1 small yellow onion, chopped

2 cups skim milk

1 medium head cauliflower, cored and roughly chopped (about 4 cups)

Salt and freshly ground black pepper

1½ cups (6 ounces) shredded 50% reduced-fat cheddar cheese, such as Cabot

½ bunch scallions (green part only), sliced thin on the diagonal

If ever there was a dynamic duo of destructive caloric forces, cheese and potatoes is it. But they taste *sooo* good together, we dive in anyway. This potato-free cheese and "potato" soup reunites the duo but tames them to a mere shadow of their former fatness. Serves 4

1. Heat a Dutch oven over medium heat. When the pot is hot, spray it with cooking spray. Add the garlic and onion. Sauté, stirring occasionally, until the garlic and onion have started to soften, about 4 minutes.

2. Add the milk and cauliflower. Season with salt and pepper to taste. Cover the pot and bring the soup to a simmer. Simmer until the cauliflower is tender, about 25 minutes.

3. Stir 1 cup of the cheddar cheese into the soup.

4. Working in batches, transfer the soup to a blender and puree until smooth. Return the soup to the pot; reheat if necessary. Season with salt and pepper to taste.

5. Ladle the soup into bowls, top with the remaining cheddar and the scallions, and serve.

NOW YOU CAN EAT THIS!

	Before	After
Fat	47 g	7 g
Calories	669	190

Protein: 19 g | Carbohydrates: 16 g
Cholesterol: 25 mg | Fiber: 3 g
Sodium: 486 mg

BROCCOLI AND CHEESE SOUP

This beautiful green soup features broccoli two ways—pureed for body and in chunks for texture. The cheese in this rendition of broccoli-cheese soup is a whisper of Parmigiano-Reggiano cheese. The real creaminess comes from yogurt. **Serves 4**

1. Heat a Dutch oven over high heat. When the pot is hot, spray it with cooking spray. Add the broccoli, onion, and garlic. Cover, and sauté the vegetables until they are almost tender, about 5 minutes. Season lightly with salt. Add the chicken broth, bring the mixture to a boil, and cook uncovered until the liquid has reduced by half, about 8 minutes.

2. Meanwhile, whisk the milk and cornstarch together in a medium bowl until thoroughly combined.

3. Whisk the cornstarch mixture into the broccoli mixture. Bring the soup to a boil and cook, stirring often, until it has thickened, about 2 minutes.

4. Pour half the contents of the pot into a blender, and puree until smooth. Pour the pureed soup back into the pot. Adjust the consistency with a little more chicken broth, if necessary.

5. Remove the pot from the heat. Stir the cheese and yogurt into the soup. Season with salt and pepper to taste, and serve.

Nonstick cooking spray

2½ cups broccoli, roughly chopped

½ medium yellow onion, chopped fine

2 garlic cloves, chopped fine

Salt

1½ cups low-fat, low-sodium chicken broth, plus extra if needed

1 cup 2% milk

1 tablespoon cornstarch

2 tablespoons grated Parmigiano-Reggiano cheese

½ cup Greek yogurt

Freshly ground black pepper

NOW YOU CAN EAT THIS!

	Before	After
Fat	34g	**5.1 g**
Calories	570	**114**

Protein: 6 g | Carbohydrates: 12 g
Cholesterol: 16 mg | Fiber: 2 g
Sodium: 460 mg

"CREAM" OF MUSHROOM SOUP

Nonstick cooking spray

One 12-ounce package sliced button mushrooms

1 small yellow onion, chopped fine

2 garlic cloves, chopped fine

Salt and freshly ground black pepper

2 cups low-fat, low-sodium chicken broth

1 can evaporated skim milk

The highest form of "cream of" soup starts out with cooked, pureed vegetables and pure, fresh cream. The second-best incarnation of that same soup winds up being pastier, with cornstarch as a thickener and the fresh cream replaced with cheaper fats, like vegetable oils. There's one more way to make cream soup, though—a way in which you get the freshest, purest, least diluted taste of the vegetables. There's no cream in this recipe—and no cornstarch, either. You still get a great creamy texture by using a lot of mushrooms and chicken broth. The key is to not let the mushroom liquor (the juice expressed by the mushrooms as they cook) evaporate, and to use a good blender to create a luxurious puree. Serves 4

1. Heat a large saucepan over high heat. When the pot is hot, spray it with cooking spray. Add the mushrooms, onion, and garlic. Sauté until the mushrooms have released most of their liquid and are starting to become tender, about 5 minutes.

2. Season the mushrooms with salt and pepper to taste. Add the chicken broth and evaporated skim milk. Cover, and bring the soup to a boil. Reduce heat and simmer until the mushrooms are completely tender, about 8 minutes.

3. Working in two batches, puree the soup in a blender until smooth. Return the soup to the pot to reheat. Season with salt and pepper to taste, and serve.

NOW YOU CAN EAT THIS!

	Before	After
Fat	46g	0.8 g
Calories	875	106

Protein: 11 g | Carbohydrates: 16 g
Cholesterol: 5 mg | Fiber: 1 g
Sodium: 534 mg

CHICKEN NOODLE SOUP

This takes a recipe that already has a reputation for promoting good health (think "Grandma's penicillin" and "nature's antibiotic") and makes it even healthier. It will cure what ails you, but you don't have to be sick to enjoy it. Serves 4

1. Bring a large pot of salted water to a boil. Cook the noodles according to the package directions, 8 to 10 minutes. Drain, and set aside.

2. While the noodles are cooking, combine the chicken broth, onion, carrots, and celery in a large saucepan, and bring to a boil over high heat. Cover, reduce the heat to medium-low, and simmer until the vegetables are tender, about 12 minutes.

3. Add the cooked noodles and the chicken to the soup. Season with salt and pepper to taste. Ladle the soup into bowls, sprinkle with the cheese and parsley, and serve.

1 ounce medium whole-wheat egg noodles

2 cups low-fat, low-sodium chicken broth

½ small yellow onion, sliced thin

1 small carrot, sliced thin on the diagonal

1 celery stalk, sliced thin on the diagonal

¾ cup shredded skinless breast meat from a rotisserie or roast chicken

Salt and freshly ground black pepper

¼ cup grated Parmigiano-Reggiano cheese

¼ cup chopped fresh flat-leaf parsley

NOW YOU CAN EAT THIS!

	Before	After
Fat	14g	**2.4g**
Calories	430	**101**

Protein: 12 g | Carbohydrates: 10 g
Cholesterol: 23 mg | Fiber: 2 g
Sodium: 675 mg

SALADS

BEET AND BLUE CHEESE SALAD WITH CRUSHED WALNUTS

2 medium red beets

6 ounces (about 10 cups) baby arugula

6 tablespoons Not So Basic Vinaigrette (page 204) or store-bought light oil and vinegar dressing, such as Ken's Steak House Healthy Options Olive Oil & Vinegar

⅓ cup chopped fresh flat-leaf parsley

Salt and freshly ground black pepper

½ cup crumbled reduced-fat blue cheese, such as Treasure Cove

¼ cup walnuts, toasted and crushed (see Healthy Tips)

This is such a great salad—especially in the fall, when beets are in season. The sweet, earthy flavor of the beets provides a nice foil for the tangy blue cheese and peppery arugula. By lightly crushing the walnuts, you need less of this healthy but high-fat nut in your salad. Sometimes it's the little things that make a big difference. **Serves 4**

1. Prick the skin of the beets with a fork. Place the beets on a microwave-safe plate and microwave on high until tender, about 12 minutes (or alternatively, wrap the beets in foil and roast them in the oven for 1 hour at 375°F). When they are cool enough to handle, peel the beets and cut them into bite-size cubes.

2. In a large bowl, combine the beets, arugula, vinaigrette, and parsley. Toss thoroughly to combine. Season with salt and pepper to taste.

3. Divide the salad among 4 salad plates. Top each salad with crumbled blue cheese and toasted walnuts, and serve.

NOW YOU CAN EAT THIS!

	Before	After
Fat	60 g	**11.1 g**
Calories	763	**166**

Protein: 7 g | Carbohydrates: 10 g
Cholesterol: 8 mg | Fiber: 3 g
Sodium: 547 mg

Healthy Tips

Walnuts are an excellent source of omega-3 essential fatty acids. Toasted and lightly crushed, they make a delicious and healthful addition to salads, steamed vegetable side dishes, and creamy pasta dishes.

To toast, spread walnut halves in a single layer on a baking sheet and toast them in a 350°F oven until they are light brown and aromatic, 7 to 10 minutes, stirring once. Let the nuts cool. To crush them, place cooled toasted walnut halves in a large bowl. Set a small bowl inside the large bowl, and apply pressure until the walnuts are cracked into small pieces.

WEDGE OF LETTUCE WITH BACON AND BLUE CHEESE

1 small head iceberg lettuce

1 small red onion, sliced very thin

1 large heirloom tomato, cut into large dice

¾ cup 3-Grams-of-Fat Blue Cheese Dressing (page 201) or Bolthouse Farms Chunky Blue Cheese Dressing

6 tablespoons crumbled reduced-fat blue cheese, such as Treasure Cove

6 tablespoons real bacon bits, such as Hormel Real Bacon Bits

Salt and freshly ground black pepper

Who doesn't love a big thick chunk of iceberg lettuce with bacon and blue cheese dressing alongside a juicy cowboy-cut ribeye? It's one of my favorite steakhouse meals. Problem is, at 700-plus calories and more than 80 grams of fat—for the salad alone!—it's a very bad bargain. Thankfully, the availability of reduced-fat blue cheese means you don't have to choose between the steak and the salad. **Serves 4**

1. Cut the iceberg lettuce into 4 wedges. Place 1 wedge on each of 4 salad plates, and top each wedge with some red onion and tomato. Drizzle each wedge with blue cheese dressing, and top it with crumbled blue cheese and bacon.

2. Season the salads with salt and pepper to taste, and serve.

NOW YOU CAN **EAT THIS!**

	Before	After
Fat	81.2g	**9.4 g**
Calories	730	**182**

Protein: 13 g | Carbohydrates: 11g
Cholesterol: 27 mg | Fiber: 2 g
Sodium: 972 mg

MIXED GREEN SALAD WITH FENNEL-TARRAGON DRESSING

A great green salad has always been a staple on my restaurant menus and on my table at home. The combination of Dijon mustard, good-quality vinegar, and olive oil gives tender green leaves their *raison d'être*. There is no olive oil in this dressing and it still tastes great. I kept the Dijon mustard in the mix because it's very low in fat—and because few ingredients can pack a punch like Dijon mustard. Yogurt, lemon juice, and aromatics like tarragon and fennel round out the dressing. You'll never again eat a green dressed with artificial-tasting, gloppy, low-fat dressing. **Serves 4**

1. To prepare the dressing: Combine the fennel, garlic, and water in a medium microwave-safe bowl, and season with salt and pepper to taste. Cover the bowl tightly with plastic wrap and microwave on high until the vegetables are completely tender, about 8 minutes.

2. In a blender, combine the cooked fennel and garlic, any remaining juices, and the lemon juice. Puree the mixture until it is smooth. Let the puree cool slightly, still in the blender. Then add the mustard, yogurt, and tarragon, and puree until smooth. Season the dressing with salt and pepper to taste; chill in the refrigerator until ready to use.

3. To prepare the salad: In a large bowl, combine the greens, radishes, tomatoes, red onion, and cucumber. Toss the salad with the dressing. Season with salt and pepper to taste, and serve.

dressing:

1 small fennel bulb, cored and roughly chopped

8 garlic cloves

¼ cup water

Salt and freshly ground black pepper

⅓ cup fresh lemon juice

3 tablespoons Dijon mustard

½ cup Greek yogurt

¼ cup fresh tarragon, whole leaves

salad:

One 7-ounce package (8 cups) green-leaf lettuce mix, such as Ready Pac Parisian

8 large radishes, sliced thin

1 cup grape tomatoes

1 small red onion, sliced thin

1 small cucumber, cut in half lengthwise and sliced into half-moons

Salt and freshly ground black pepper

NOW YOU CAN **EAT THIS!**

	Before	After
Fat	27 g	**3.1 g**
Calories	350	**119**

Protein: 4 g | Carbohydrates: 19 g
Cholesterol: 8 mg | Fiber: 5 g
Sodium: 638 mg

TOMATO AND MOZZARELLA SALAD

2 large red heirloom tomatoes, cut into large dice

1 small red onion, sliced thin

6 ounces fresh mozzarella, cut into large dice

3 tablespoons red wine vinegar

1 tablespoon extra-virgin olive oil

¾ cup chopped fresh basil

Salt and freshly ground black pepper

The Italian name for this salad is *insalata caprese,* and it's a shining example of the brilliance of Italian cuisine: a few fresh, simple ingredients at the peak of their season combined to produce exceptionally complex flavors. It hails from Capri, a small island off the coast of Naples in the region of Campagna, where my family comes from. Buy only the best mozzarella, tomatoes, basil, and olive oil you can find to make this salad. It may be naturally fresh and healthful, but I have kept fat and calories to a minimum by keeping the olive oil to a minimum—only 1 tablespoon for 4 servings. **Serves 4**

In a large bowl, toss the tomatoes, onion, mozzarella, vinegar, olive oil, and basil. Season the salad with salt and pepper to taste. Serve immediately, or chill in the refrigerator until serving time.

NOW YOU CAN **EAT THIS!**

	Before	After
Fat	42g	**13.1 g**
Calories	450	**184**

Protein: 10 g | Carbohydrates: 6 g
Cholesterol: 34 mg | Fiber: 1 g
Sodium: 417 mg

COBB SALAD

Cobb Salad gets its name from Robert Cobb, owner of the Brown Derby restaurant in Los Angeles and first cousin of baseball great Ty Cobb. The story goes that he was browsing through the refrigerator late one night, looking for a snack, and could only find bits and pieces of leftovers—which he chopped up and turned into a salad. The rest is history. Here's a version of Cobb Salad that was put together with a little more thought—and a lot fewer calories. **Serves 4**

1. Divide the lettuce evenly among 4 large dinner plates. Arrange the sliced chicken on top of the lettuce. Scatter the tomatoes and scallions over the chicken, and arrange the avocado slices on top of the salads. Season with salt and pepper to taste.

2. Scatter the bacon bits and blue cheese over the salads. Drizzle with salad dressing, and serve.

9 ounces (about 10 cups) sweet lettuce mix

8 ounces grilled chicken breast, sliced

1 large red heirloom tomato, cut into medium dice

3 scallions (white and green parts), sliced thin on the diagonal

½ ripe avocado, sliced thin

Salt and freshly ground black pepper

¼ cup real bacon bits, such as Hormel Real Bacon Bits

½ cup crumbled reduced-fat blue cheese, such as Treasure Cove

6 tablespoons Not So Basic Vinaigrette (page 204) or store-bought light oil and vinegar dressing, such as Ken's Steak House Healthy Options Olive Oil & Vinegar

NOW YOU CAN EAT THIS!

	Before	After
Fat	71 g	**11.3 g**
Calories	1,090	**235**

Protein: 24 g | Carbohydrates: 11 g
Cholesterol: 52 mg | Fiber: 3 g
Sodium: 1,081 mg

CHINESE CHICKEN SALAD

I remember the first time I had "Chinese" chicken salad. It was at a trendy West Hollywood spot on Sunset Boulevard, and it could have been/should have been a lot better than it was. Fried noodles only do not a Chinese chicken salad make. In this recipe, textured vegetable protein, or TVP, replaces the noodles for crunch and bite. TVP is made from defatted soy flour, a by-product of making soybean oil. It's high in protein and low in fat. TVP flakes are available in the health-food aisle of most major supermarkets. **Serves 4**

1. In a large bowl, whisk together the Asian sauce, lime juice, and chili garlic sauce. Add the shredded chicken, red cabbage, snow peas, cilantro, and sesame seeds. Toss the salad to combine. Chill in the refrigerator until serving time, up to 6 hours.

2. If desired, sprinkle the salad with textured vegetable protein right before serving.

1 cup Rockin' Asian Stir-Fry Sauce (page 210) or store-bought low-fat, low-calorie Asian sauce

Juice from 1 lime

1 teaspoon chili garlic sauce

Shredded skinless breast meat from 1 rotisserie or roast chicken

4 cups shredded red cabbage

4 ounces snow peas, strings removed

½ cup chopped fresh cilantro

2 tablespoons black sesame seeds

6 tablespoons textured vegetable protein (TVP), such as Bob's Red Mill (optional)

NOW YOU CAN **EAT THIS!**

	Before	After
Fat	26.1 g	**5.5 g**
Calories	801	**221**

Protein: 25 g | Carbohydrates: 19 g
Cholesterol: 44 mg | Fiber: 5 g
Sodium: 1,424 mg

GRILLED CHICKEN CAESAR SALAD

5 slices whole-wheat baguette (cut 1 inch thick)

3 large garlic cloves: 1 whole, 2 minced

Salt and freshly ground black pepper

4 chicken cutlets (2 ounces each), pounded thin

Nonstick olive oil cooking spray

2 tablespoons fresh lemon juice

5 tablespoons Rocco's Magnificent Mayonnaise (page 200) or store-bought low-fat mayonnaise, such as Hellmann's Low-Fat Mayonnaise Dressing

2 teaspoons Dijon mustard

½ cup grated Parmigiano-Reggiano cheese

One 9-ounce package (about 7 cups) cut romaine lettuce

This dish has become a staple on the American menu. From McDonalds to gastro-pubs to fine-dining restaurants, everyone has their own version. I'd venture to say mine is among the tastiest and healthiest out there. **Serves 4**

1. Preheat the oven to 375°F. Line a baking sheet with foil.

2. To make the croutons, rub the baguette slices with the whole garlic clove. Using a serrated knife, cut the bread into 1-inch cubes. Place the cubes on the prepared baking sheet, and season them with salt and pepper to taste. Toast the cubes in the oven until they are golden brown and crunchy, about 10 minutes. Let cool.

3. While the croutons are cooling, preheat a grill or grill pan over high heat. Season the chicken with salt and pepper, and spray it lightly with olive oil spray.

4. Grill the chicken until just cooked through, about 1½ minutes per side. Place 1 cutlet on each of 4 large dinner plates.

5. In a large bowl, combine the minced garlic, lemon juice, mayonnaise, Dijon mustard, and half of the grated cheese. Add the lettuce and croutons to the bowl. Season the salad with salt and pepper to taste, and toss thoroughly.

6. Pile equal portions of salad on top of the chicken, mounding it high. Sprinkle each salad with some of the remaining cheese, and serve.

NOW YOU CAN **EAT THIS!**

	Before	After
Fat	64g	**6.1g**
Calories	850	**202**

Protein: 20 g | Carbohydrates: 15 g
Cholesterol: 45 mg | Fiber: 3 g
Sodium: 600 mg

LEMONY SHRIMP SALAD

A healthy amount of celery gives this traditionally rich seafood salad a good bit of crunch. The lightened-up lemony mayonnaise dressing would be delicious with any cold, steamed, or poached seafood, including crab, scallops, and lobster. **Serves 4**

1. Bring a large pot of salted water to a boil. Turn off the heat and stir the shrimp into the water. Poach the shrimp, off the heat, until they are just cooked through, about 2 minutes; drain. Spread the shrimp in a single layer on a large plate or dish. Chill in the refrigerator until very cold, about 1 hour.

2. Whisk the mayonnaise, lemon zest, lemon juice, and tarragon together in a large bowl. Add the chilled shrimp, along with the celery and red onion. Toss gently to combine. Season with salt and pepper to taste. Serve immediately, or chill covered in the refrigerator for up to 24 hours.

12 ounces large shrimp, peeled and deveined, cut in half crosswise

½ cup Rocco's Magnificent Mayonnaise (page 200) or store-bought low-fat mayonnaise, such as Hellmann's Low-Fat Mayonnaise Dressing

Grated zest from 1 lemon

2 tablespoons fresh lemon juice

2 tablespoons chopped fresh tarragon

3 large celery stalks, sliced thin on the diagonal

1 small red onion, chopped fine

Salt and freshly ground black pepper

NOW YOU CAN **EAT THIS!**

	Before	After
Fat	27 g	**5.8 g**
Calories	320	**175**

Protein: 19 g | Carbohydrates: 12 g
Cholesterol: 135 mg | Fiber: 1 g
Sodium: 707 mg

NIÇOISE SALAD

6 ounces haricots verts or thin string beans

3 large hard-boiled eggs, peeled

1 ounce (¼ cup) pitted Niçoise or kalamata olives, roughly chopped

6 tablespoons Not So Basic Vinaigrette (page 204) or store-bought light oil and vinegar dressing, such as Ken's Steak House Healthy Options Olive Oil & Vinegar

⅓ cup chopped fresh flat-leaf parsley

One 6.5-ounce package (about 8 cups) sweet lettuce mix

1 cup grape tomatoes

Three 5-ounce cans chunk light tuna packed in water, drained

Classic *salade Niçoise* from the South of France is a relatively light dish to start. With only 477 calories per serving in the original, I was challenged on this one. There was wiggle room, though: My version trims a bit here and there by calling for canned tuna packed in water, egg whites only (instead of whole eggs), a lighter vinaigrette than the traditional anchovy-based dressing, and more greens. **Serves 4**

1. Bring a large pot of salted water to a boil. Add the haricots verts and cook until just tender, about 4 minutes. Using a slotted spoon or a skimmer, transfer the haricots verts to a bowl of ice water to stop the cooking process and preserve the color. When they are cold, drain the haricots verts and reserve them.

2. Cut the hard-boiled eggs in half; remove and discard the yolks. Slice the egg whites and set them aside.

3. In a small bowl, mix the olives with the vinaigrette and parsley.

4. To assemble the salads, divide the lettuce among 4 large dinner plates. Scatter the grape tomatoes and tuna over the lettuce. Divide the sliced egg whites and haricots verts among the 4 salads. Drizzle with the vinaigrette, and serve.

NOW YOU CAN EAT THIS!

	Before	After
Fat	28g	**5.3 g**
Calories	477	**193**

Protein: 29 g | Carbohydrates: 11 g
Cholesterol: 56 mg | Fiber: 4 g
Sodium: 775 mg

Healthy Tips

It's long been established that the more flavorful a food is, the less you need to eat to feel satisfied. It has more recently been established that there are "super foods" that contain very high levels of nutrients. For a low-calorie "super food" snack, try water-packed canned sardines (the best ones come from Portugal) on sliced ripe tomatoes seasoned with Tabasco.

SKINNY CHEF'S SALAD

Never trust a skinny chef—or one who serves you an 800- to 1,400-calorie chef's salad! If you think you're being good when you order this dish, think again. Given the exceedingly large quantity of deli meats, the Russian dressing, and the boiled eggs, you might as well eat a Big Mac. This version, however, really *is* a skinny salad. It calls for egg whites only, reduced-fat cheddar, and a reduced-fat full-flavor Russian dressing of my own creation. **Serves 4**

1. Cut the hard-boiled eggs in half; remove and discard the yolks. Dice the egg whites.

2. Divide the lettuce among 4 large dinner plates. Top with the sliced egg whites, ham, turkey, cheese, tomatoes, and cucumber. Season with salt and pepper to taste. Drizzle the dressing on top, and serve.

4 large hard-boiled eggs, peeled

9 ounces (about 10 cups) sweet butter lettuce mix

4 ounces ham, diced

12 ounces thickly sliced turkey breast (from the deli counter), cut into wide strips

1 cup shredded 75% reduced-fat cheddar cheese, such as Cabot

1 cup grape tomatoes, sliced in half

1 small cucumber, halved lengthwise and sliced into ¼-inch-thick half-moons (about 1½ cups)

Salt and freshly ground black pepper

½ cup "Russian Island" Dressing (page 203) or store-bought reduced-fat Russian dressing

NOW YOU CAN **EAT THIS!**

	Before	After
Fat	61 g	**7.6 g**
Calories	860	**245**

Protein: 36 g | Carbohydrates: 13 g
Cholesterol: 71 mg | Fiber: 3 g
Sodium: 1,848 mg

SANDWICHES
AND PIZZA

CHARRED BEEF BURGERS WITH BABA GHANOUSH

The Big Mac is a great burger—juicy, delicious, and an icon of American culture. So how do I re-create the grandeur of the Big Mac while stripping away a lot of the fat and calories that go with it? First replace the bun with a nutrient-rich, high-fiber sprouted-grain hamburger bun. My "special sauce" is made with charred eggplant and low-fat yogurt, and the beef is extra-lean. A little low-fat Russian dressing, which I consider to be *my* special sauce, gives it some zest—and all the rest is healthy on its own. (No cheese needed.) **Serves 4**

1. Char the eggplant over an open flame, rotating it often to cook evenly, about 20 minutes. The skin should be completely blackened and the flesh should be cooked through. Place the eggplant in a bowl, cover it tightly with plastic wrap (to steam off the skin), and set it aside for 5 to 10 minutes. Then remove the charred skin with a paper towel, leaving the flesh behind. Chop the eggplant with a knife until it is a thick and chunky puree. Mix the eggplant and the yogurt together in a bowl, and season it with salt and pepper to taste.

2. Preheat a grill or grill pan over high heat.

3. Split the buns in half, and spray the split surfaces lightly with cooking spray. Season the burger patties with salt and pepper to taste. Place the buns, cut sides down, and the burgers on the grill. Allow the buns to char slightly, and then transfer them to a platter. Cook the burgers for about 2½ minutes per side for rare.

4. To assemble the burgers, spread the bottom buns with some of the eggplant mixture. Place the burgers on top, and then top each burger with some of the Russian dressing. Pile the tomato, onion, and lettuce on the burgers, and set the bun tops in place. Serve.

1 medium eggplant

2 tablespoons 5% Greek yogurt

Salt and freshly ground black pepper

4 Ezekiel 4:9 Sprouted Whole-Grain Flourless Burger Buns

Nonfat cooking spray

12 ounces 90% lean ground beef, formed into 4 patties

½ cup "Russian Island" Dressing (page 203) or store-bought reduced-fat Russian dressing

4 slices heirloom tomato

4 slices red onion

4 leaves romaine lettuce, broken in half

NOW YOU CAN **EAT THIS!**

	Before	After
Fat	29 g	**7.4 g**
Calories	540	**341**

Protein: 30 g | Carbohydrates: 38 g
Cholesterol: 56 mg | Fiber: 7 g
Sodium: 773 mg

OVER THE TOP GRILLED CHEESE

8 pieces thin-sliced European whole-grain bread, such as Rubschlager

4 ounces 75% reduced-fat cheddar, such as Cabot, shredded

2 tablespoons sugar-free orange marmalade

4 slices 2% reduced-fat-milk cheese, such as Borden's 2% Milk Reduced Fat Sharp Singles

As basic as a grilled cheese sandwich is, there are ways to make it badly (I've had a few of those) and ways to make it beautifully. This is how it should be: The bread should be toasted and crispy (hence the broiling), the cheese should be warm and melted but not running out of the sides, and there should be a little something extra to truly take it over the top. Here, a little orange marmalade adds a touch of sweetness to the otherwise savory elements. **Serves 4**

1. Preheat the broiler on high.

2. Meanwhile, assemble the sandwiches: Lay 4 slices of bread on a work surface. Divide the shredded cheddar among the 4 pieces of bread. Place ½ tablespoon of the orange marmalade on top of the shredded cheese. Place the cheese slices on top of the marmalade. Top each sandwich with the remaining bread, pressing lightly to spread the marmalade.

3. Transfer the sandwiches to a baking sheet, and broil until they are golden brown and crispy and the cheese is melted, about 4 minutes per side. Cut each sandwich in half, and serve.

NOW YOU CAN **EAT THIS!**

	Before	After
Fat	47 g	**8.5** g
Calories	650	**295**

Protein: 23 g | Carbohydrates: 35 g
Cholesterol: 20 mg | Fiber: 8 g
Sodium: 760 mg

TUNA BURGERS WITH BASIL AND PEPPERONCINI MAYONNAISE

In preparing these burgers, use a food processor to chop the raw tuna, but be careful not to overdo it. Pulse just enough to chop it—too much action can toughen the fish, and you'll wind up with a dry burger instead of a juicy, flavorful one. **Serves 4**

1. Place the tuna in a food processor and pulse on and off for a few seconds, until the tuna is chopped but not overly processed; you don't want it to be pureed.

2. Preheat a grill or grill pan over high heat.

3. While the grill is heating, combine the tuna, salmon, and 2 tablespoons of the mayonnaise in a medium bowl. Using your hands, gently form the fish mixture into 4 burgers. Season them with salt and pepper and spray them lightly with nonstick cooking spray.

4. Grill the burgers until they are seared on the outside but still a little rare in the center, about 2 minutes per side. Transfer them to a serving platter and tent it with foil to keep them warm.

5. While the burgers are cooking, combine the basil, pepperoncini, and the remaining mayonnaise in a medium bowl. Season the mixture with salt and pepper to taste. Set it aside.

6. Split the buns and place them on the grill or grill pan, cut side down. Lightly char the buns, 1 to 2 minutes. Remove the buns from the heat and place them on a work surface.

7. Spread the mayonnaise mixture evenly over the top and bottom halves of the buns. Top the bottom half of each bun with a tuna burger and a tomato slice. Pile some shredded lettuce on top of the tomato, cover with the bun top, and serve.

12 ounces sushi-grade tuna, cut into chunks

4 ounces smoked salmon, chopped

½ cup Rocco's Magnificent Mayonnaise (page 200) or store-bought low-fat mayonnaise, such as Hellmann's Low-Fat Mayonnaise Dressing

Salt and freshly ground black pepper

Nonstick cooking spray

¼ cup chopped fresh basil

6 large jarred pepperoncini, chopped fine

4 sprouted-grain hamburger buns, such as Ezekiel 4:9

4 slices heirloom tomato

4 leaves romaine lettuce, shredded

NOW YOU CAN **EAT THIS!**

	Before	After
Fat	48g	**5.9 g**
Calories	770	**342**

Protein: 35 g | Carbohydrates: 39 g
Cholesterol: 51 mg | Fiber: 7 g
Sodium: 1,071 mg

SHRIMP PO' BOYS
WITH SPICY MAYO

½ cup whole-wheat flour

2 cups whole-wheat panko breadcrumbs, such as Ian's All-Natural

3 egg whites

8 ounces large shrimp, peeled and deveined

Salt

½ cup Rocco's Magnificent Mayonnaise (page 200) or store-bought low-fat mayonnaise, such as Hellmann's Low-Fat Mayonnaise Dressing

2 tablespoons Tabasco sauce

4 sprouted-grain buns, such as Ezekiel 4:9, toasted or broiled

4 leaves shredded romaine lettuce

½ cup jarred roasted red pepper strips

Po' boys are a kind of sub sandwich from the sultry state of Louisiana, consisting of fried meat or fish served on a crispy French-style baguette. Traditionally they are made with fried shrimp or oysters, though soft-shell crabs, catfish, crawfish, Louisiana hot sausage, and roast beef have been known to make an appearance. Served hot, the shellfish, fish, or meat is dressed with some combination of lettuce, tomatoes, peppers, pickles, onions, and mustard or a spicy mayo. In this version the fat and calories are reduced to a fraction of the original by faux frying the shrimp, using low-fat mayonnaise, and replacing the traditional white-flour baguette with sprouted-grain bread. **Serves 4**

1. Preheat the oven to 450°F. Place a wire rack on a baking sheet and set it aside.

2. Place the flour in a shallow dish. Place the panko in another shallow dish. In a medium bowl, whip the egg whites with a whisk until they are extremely foamy but not quite holding peaks.

3. Working in batches, dredge the shrimp in the flour, shaking off any excess. Add the shrimp to the egg whites; toss to coat completely. Then add the shrimp to the panko and turn to coat them completely.

4. Place the shrimp on the wire rack, and season them generously with salt. Bake until the breading is golden and crispy and the shrimp are cooked through, about 8 minutes.

5. Meanwhile, stir the mayonnaise and Tabasco sauce together in a small bowl. Spread the cut sides of each bun generously with the mayonnaise mixture. Top the bottom half of each bun with lettuce and red pepper strips.

6. Pile the shrimp on top of the peppers. Place the bun tops over the shrimp, and serve.

NOW YOU CAN EAT THIS!

	Before	After
Fat	57 g	**5.2 g**
Calories	837	**342**

Protein: 24 g | Carbohydrates: 53 g
Cholesterol: 71 mg | Fiber: 8 g
Sodium: 813 mg

TUNA MELT

Two 6-ounce cans solid white albacore tuna packed in water, well drained

2 medium celery stalks, chopped fine

6 tablespoons Rocco's Magnificent Mayonnaise (page 200) or store-bought reduced-fat mayonnaise, such as Hellmann's Low-Fat Mayonnaise Dressing

Salt and freshly ground black pepper

8 slices whole-grain European-style bread, such as Rubschlager

3 ounces 75% reduced-fat cheddar, such as Cabot, sliced

Nonfat cooking spray

This sandwich is so old-school—and I love it. Using water-packed tuna and a reasonable amount of low-fat mayonnaise takes this diner-food classic off the "Do Not Eat" list. **Serves 4**

1. Heat 2 large nonstick sauté pans over medium-low heat.

2. Meanwhile, in a medium bowl, mix together the tuna, celery, and mayonnaise. Season the mixture with salt and pepper to taste.

3. Lay 4 slices of bread on a work surface. Divide the sliced cheese among the bread slices, and then divide the tuna salad among the bread slices. Top each sandwich with another piece of bread.

4. When the pans are hot, spray them well with cooking spray. Add 2 sandwiches to each pan, and spray the top slices of bread lightly with the cooking spray. Weight the sandwiches down with plates that are slightly smaller than the circumference of the pans. Cook the sandwiches until the bread is golden brown and crispy and the cheese has melted, about 4 minutes per side. (Alternatively, you can use a panini press to cook the sandwiches.) Cut the sandwiches in half, and serve.

NOW YOU CAN **EAT THIS!**

	Before	After
Fat	92g	**7.1g**
Calories	1,230	**343**

Protein: 36 g | Carbohydrates: 33 g
Cholesterol: 48 mg | Fiber: 6 g
Sodium: 909 mg

SMOKED TURKEY REUBEN

Some say the Reuben—corned beef brisket, Russian dressing, Swiss cheese, sauerkraut, bread—was invented by an Omaha grocer named Reuben Kulakofsky to provide sustenance to participants in a late-night poker game. This reformed version was invented to help you eat better. (Following that logic, don't stay up late playing poker, either.)
Serves 4

1. Place the sauerkraut in a microwave-safe bowl and cover it with plastic wrap. Microwave on high power until it is hot, about 2 minutes.

2. Heat 2 nonstick sauté pans over medium-low heat.

3. Lay 4 slices of the bread on a work surface, and spread each slice with 1 tablespoon of the "Russian Island" Dressing. Top each slice with a slice of cheese, and then a portion of the smoked turkey. Divide the warm sauerkraut among the 4 sandwiches, and spoon the remaining Russian dressing over the sauerkraut. Finally, top the sandwiches with the remaining slices of bread.

4. Spray the sauté pans generously with cooking spray, and place 2 sandwiches in each pan. Weigh the sandwiches down with plates that are just slightly smaller than the circumference of the pans. Cook the sandwiches for about 4 minutes per side, or until the bread is crispy and golden brown and the cheese has melted. Cut the sandwiches in half, and serve.

12 ounces sauerkraut, very well drained

8 slices sprouted-grain bread, such as Ezekiel 4:9

½ cup "Russian Island" Dressing (page 203) or store-bought low-calorie Russian or Thousand Island Dressing

4 slices reduced-fat Swiss cheese (1 ounce each)

8 ounces sliced smoked turkey (from the deli counter)

Nonfat cooking spray

NOW YOU CAN EAT THIS!

	Before	After
Fat	60g	**8.9 g**
Calories	920	**335**

Protein: 26 g | Carbohydrates: 37 g
Cholesterol: 42 mg | Fiber: 9 g
Sodium: 1,539 mg

PHILLY CHEESESTEAK

Is it the bun, the beef, or the processed cheese that makes a Philly cheesesteak America's most famous hero sandwich? Some say all three are equally important. Suffice it to say that from my research, there will never be agreement on this issue. We can all agree, though, that this whole-grain, low-fat sandwich is a different kind of hero.

Serves 4

1. Heat a large nonstick sauté pan over medium-high heat. When the pan is hot, spray it well with cooking spray and add the onion and pepper. Season with salt and pepper to taste, cover the pan, and cook, stirring occasionally, until the vegetables have softened, about 12 minutes.

2. Meanwhile, heat a grill pan over high heat. When the pan is hot, split the buns in half and place them on the pan, cut side down. Allow the buns to char a little, about 1 to 2 minutes. Remove the buns from the grill pan and set them aside.

3. Combine the beef broth, chicken broth, and sliced roast beef in a medium sauté pan, using a fork to separate the roast beef slices. Heat the beef gently over medium heat until the broth is hot but not boiling. Drain the beef, reserving the broth.

4. Divide the beef among the bottom halves of the toasted buns. Top each sandwich with 1½ slices of the cheese. Top the cheese with the hot onion-pepper mixture, and then the ketchup. Close the sandwiches with the bun tops, and serve them with the warm broth for dipping.

Nonfat cooking spray

1 large Vidalia onion, sliced thin

1 large green bell pepper, seeded and sliced thin

Salt and freshly ground black pepper

4 sprouted-grain hamburger buns, such as Ezekiel 4:9, or 4 whole-wheat buns

¾ cup low-fat, low-sodium beef broth

¾ cup low-fat, low-sodium chicken broth

8 ounces sliced lean roast beef (from the deli counter)

6 slices 2% reduced-fat-milk cheese, such as Borden 2% Milk Reduced-Fat Sharp Singles

6 tablespoons reduced-sugar ketchup, such as Heinz

NOW YOU CAN **EAT THIS!**

	Before	After
Fat	50g	**7.6 g**
Calories	902	**344**

Protein: 27 g | Carbohydrates: 44 g
Cholesterol: 40 mg | Fiber: 7 g
Sodium: 1,487 mg

SLOPPY JOE

2 large garlic cloves

1 small yellow onion, quartered

1 small green bell pepper, seeded and cut into large chunks

Nonstick cooking spray

Salt and freshly ground black pepper

12 ounces ground turkey breast

Scant ¾ cup reduced-sugar ketchup, such as Heinz

⅔ cup water

2 tablespoons Worcestershire sauce

1 teaspoon chili powder

4 sprouted-grain hamburger buns, such as Ezekiel 4:9

It may have been easy to reduce the sugar, fat, calories, and carbs in these sandwiches, but when it comes to the sloppy part, you're on your own. Eat with lots of napkins. **Serves 4**

1. Heat a large nonstick sauté pan over medium-high heat.

2. While the pan is heating, combine the garlic, onion, and bell pepper in the bowl of a food processor, and pulse until finely chopped.

3. When the pan is hot, spray it with cooking spray. Add the chopped vegetables, and season with salt and pepper to taste. Cook, stirring occasionally, until the mixture is fragrant and and the vegetables are tender, about 4 minutes.

4. Add the turkey to the pan and cook, stirring with a wooden spoon to break it up. Season with salt and pepper, continuing to break it up with a spoon as it cooks. When the turkey is cooked through (after about 4 minutes), add the ketchup, water, Worcestershire sauce, and chili powder. Bring the mixture to a simmer, stirring occasionally.

5. Toast the hamburger buns in a toaster oven. Season the meat mixture with salt and pepper to taste, if desired. Divide the meat mixture among the buns, and serve.

NOW YOU CAN EAT THIS!

	Before	After
Fat	27.1 g	**2.4 g**
Calories	635	**297**

Protein: 29 g | Carbohydrates: 42 g
Cholesterol: 41 mg | Fiber: 7 g
Sodium: 461 mg

BLT

Using turkey bacon would have been the shortest route to making over this classic sandwich—but when bacon is the first ingredient in the name of a dish, you have to figure out a way to use the real thing. So I made over the mayonnaise instead. **Serves 4**

1. Heat 2 nonstick sauté pans over medium heat. When the pans are hot, add the bacon and cook until crisp, about 5 minutes per side. Thoroughly drain the bacon on paper towels; set aside.

2. Meanwhile, toast the bread in a toaster or toaster oven until golden brown.

3. Lay the toast on a work surface. Spread each piece with mayonnaise. Top 4 toast slices with the bacon. Add the lettuce and the tomato slices. Place the remaining toast slices on top, mayonnaise side down. Secure the sandwiches with toothpicks, if desired. Cut them in half, and serve.

16 slices reduced-fat bacon

8 slices sprouted-grain bread, such as Ezekiel 4:9

½ cup Rocco's Magnificent Mayonnaise (page 200) or store-bought reduced-fat mayonnaise, such as Hellmann's Low-Fat Mayonnaise Dressing

6 large romaine lettuce leaves, washed and torn in half

8 thick slices red heirloom tomato

NOW YOU CAN EAT THIS!

	Before	After
Fat	42g	**13.3 g**
Calories	781	**348**

Protein: 18 g | Carbohydrates: 35 g
Cholesterol: 66 mg | Fiber: 7 g
Sodium: 1,189 mg

DEEP-DISH PIZZA

This pizza is so good, I could eat it every day—and at 218 calories per serving, that wouldn't be a bad thing! It takes more effort than most of the dishes in this book, but few things are as satisfying as making your own pizza from scratch. If you are deterred by the concept of making your own dough, there are alternatives. Boboli makes a very good prepared whole-wheat crust (although it is loaded with sugar and is made from a mix of whole-wheat and white flours, unlike this all-whole-wheat version). Mix and match the toppings for variety.
Serves 6

½ teaspoon molasses

¾ cup warm water (110°F)

1½ teaspoons active dry yeast

½ teaspoon salt

1¾ cups whole-wheat flour, plus extra for rolling and kneading

Nonstick olive oil spray

1 tablespoon cornmeal

⅔ cup Rocco's How Low Can You Go Low-Fat Marinara Sauce (page 206) or store-bought low-fat marinara sauce

1 cup shredded reduced-fat mozzarella cheese, such as Weight Watchers

1 portobello mushroom, sliced very thin

2 ounces reduced-fat pepperoni, such as Carando

½ cup torn fresh basil leaves

2 tablespoons grated Parmigiano-Reggiano cheese

1. In a large bowl, dissolve the molasses in the warm water. Sprinkle the yeast over the liquid and let stand until foamy, about 10 minutes.

2. Stir the salt into the yeast mixture. Then stir in the flour until the dough starts to come together. Turn the dough out onto a work surface that has been sprinkled lightly with flour. Knead the dough until it becomes smooth and elastic, about 5 minutes. Place the dough in a large bowl that has been sprayed with olive oil spray; cover it loosely with a clean kitchen towel. Let the dough sit in a warm place until it has doubled in size, about 1 hour.

3. Gently punch the dough down. Spray a 7×11-inch baking sheet with olive oil spray, and then sprinkle it with the cornmeal. Using your fingertips, spread the dough out to completely cover the baking sheet. Spray the surface of the dough lightly with olive oil spray. Cover it lightly with plastic wrap, and let it sit in a warm place until the dough has doubled in size, about 30 minutes.

4. Place a pizza stone in the oven and preheat the oven to 500°F.

5. Place the baking sheet on top of the stone, and bake until the crust is golden brown, crunchy, and cooked through, about 12 minutes. Remove the baking sheet from the oven.

6. Turn the broiler on high.

(*continued on next page*)

NOW YOU CAN **EAT THIS!**

	Before	After
Fat	42g	**5 g**
Calories	610	**218**

Protein: 13 g | Carbohydrates: 31 g
Cholesterol: 23 mg | Fiber: 6 g
Sodium: 542 mg

7. Spread the marinara sauce evenly over the crust. Top the pizza with the mozzarella, mushroom, pepperoni, basil, and cheese. Place the baking sheet on the pizza stone and broil until the cheese is bubbly and beginning to brown, 5 to 6 minutes. Cut the pizza into 6 slices, and serve.

Per serving:

If you're feeling creative, you can add these toppings to the pizza:	Fat	Calories
1 ounce (¼ cup) chopped kalamata olives	1.3 g	15
1 ounce (3 tablespoons) chopped anchovies	0.46 g	9.9
2 ounces (½ cup) reduced-fat provolone cheese	1.7 g	25
3 ounces (½ cup) diced ham	1.25 g	25
3 ounces (¾ cup) crumbled cooked turkey sausage	1.15 g	22

Healthy Tips

Alcohol is the epitome of empty calories. Although even in moderation it may taste good and temporarily lighten your mood, it can weigh your body down. Low-calorie powdered iced tea mixes stirred into chilled sparkling water make a fun but zero-calorie, alcohol-free sparkling beverage.

INDIVIDUAL EXTRA-CRISPY THIN-CRUST PIZZAS

If you love thin-crust pizza (I am one of you), after you taste this version, you will never buy premade crusts again. Once baked, these crusts hold well at room temperature for several days if lightly covered with a tea towel—and hold very well in the refrigerator, covered with plastic wrap, for up to a week. Make a batch on Saturday for later in the week. Please note: This is a very generous portion—you might be full after eating just half of one personal-size pie. **Serves 6**

1. In a large bowl, dissolve the molasses in the warm water. Sprinkle the yeast over the liquid and let stand until foamy, about 10 minutes.

2. Stir the salt into the yeast mixture. Then stir in the flour until the dough starts to come together. Turn the dough out onto a work surface that has been sprinkled lightly with flour. Knead the dough until it becomes smooth and elastic, about 5 minutes. Place the dough in a large bowl that has been sprayed with the olive oil spray; cover it loosely with a clean kitchen towel. Let the dough sit in a warm place until it has doubled in size, about 1 hour.

3. Turn dough out onto a lightly floured surface, and divide it into 6 equal pieces. Form each piece into a tight ball by rolling it in the palm of your hand until the edges have rounded. Spray a baking sheet with olive oil spray. Arrange the dough balls a few inches apart on the prepared baking sheet. Cover them with plastic wrap and let rise until doubled, about 45 minutes.

4. Preheat the oven to 500°F or its highest setting. Place a pizza stone in the oven and heat it for 20 minutes, until it is very hot.

5. Dust a wooden pizza peel with the cornmeal. On a lightly floured surface roll a ball of dough with a rolling pin until it will not stretch any further. Drape it over both of your fists, and gently pull the edges outward while rotating the crust. When the crust has reached the desired size—about 8 to 10 inches in diameter—place it on the prepared peel. Prick the dough in about 8 places with a fork.

(*continued on next page*)

½ teaspoon molasses

¾ cup warm water (110°F)

1½ teaspoons active dry yeast

½ teaspoon salt

1¾ cups whole-wheat flour, plus extra for rolling and kneading

Nonstick olive oil spray

1 tablespoon cornmeal

¾ cup Rocco's How Low Can You Go Low-Fat Marinara Sauce (page 206) or store-bought low-fat marinara sauce

½ cup torn fresh basil leaves

1½ cups shredded reduced-fat mozzarella cheese, such as Weight Watchers

2 tablespoons grated Parmigiano-Reggiano cheese

NOW YOU CAN **EAT THIS!**

	Before	After
Fat	42g	**5.2 g**
Calories	610	**210**

Protein: 11 g | Carbohydrates: 30 g
Cholesterol: 17 mg | Fiber: 5 g
Sodium: 423 mg

6. Slide the dough onto the hot pizza stone in the oven, and bake it for 2 to 3 minutes. Then flip it over and bake until it is very crisp, about 2 minutes. Set the crust aside. Repeat with the remaining dough.

7. Turn the broiler to high.

8. Spread about 2 tablespoons of the marinara sauce on each crust, leaving a ½-inch border. Top with the basil. Mix the cheeses together in a bowl, and sprinkle the mixture over the pizzas. One at a time, slide the pizzas back onto the pizza stone. Broil until the cheese is golden brown and bubbling and the crust is brown and crispy, 4 to 5 minutes.

9. Cut the pizzas into wedges, if desired, and serve.

Per serving:

If you're feeling creative, you can add any of these toppings to each pizza:	Fat	Calories
⅓ cup Cento Sautéed Sweet Peppers	3 g	50
1 ounce (2 tablespoons) part-skim ricotta	2.2 g	39
1 meatball (see page 178)	4.5 g	85
½ portobello mushroom, sliced (1 cup)	0.1 g	11

"As a chef, I'm constantly tasting all kinds of dishes. Gaining 30-plus pounds over the last decade unfortunately came with the territory. Eating the foods in this book, however, has helped me shed the extra pounds without sacrificing the foods I love."

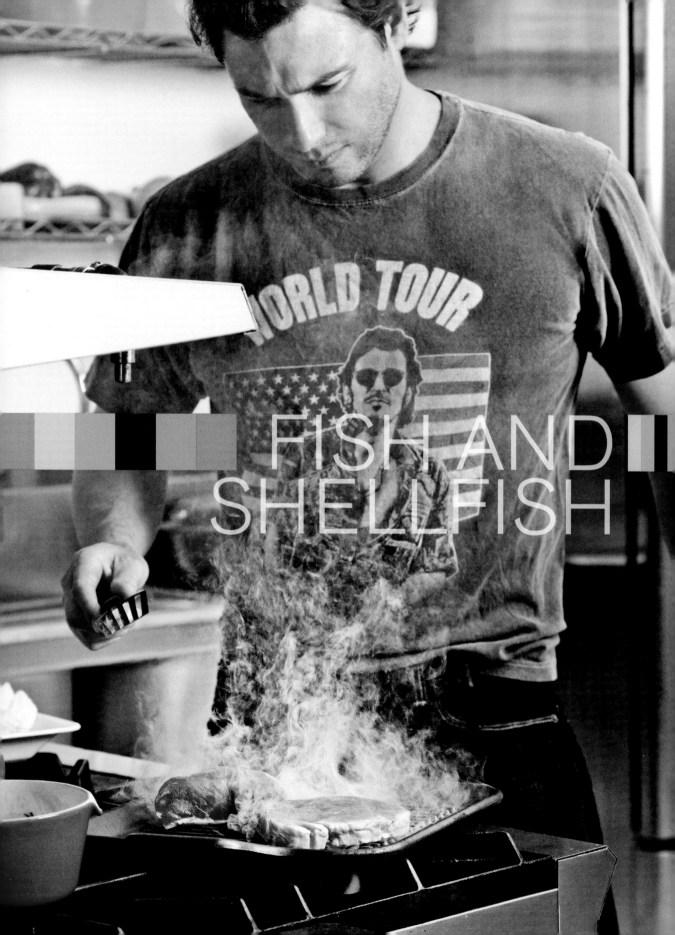

FISH AND
SHELLFISH

SALMON WITH MUSTARD CRUST AND SAUTÉED SPINACH

Nonstick cooking spray

1 small red onion, sliced very thin

⅓ cup Dijon mustard

1 small navel orange, peeled and cut into segments

Salt and freshly ground black pepper

4 salmon fillets (4 ounces each)

2 garlic cloves, sliced very thin

2 tablespoons real bacon bits, such as Hormel Real Bacon Bits

12 ounces baby spinach

Almost all of the fat in this dish comes from the salmon. Fish fat is a "good" fat, rich in omega-3 fatty acids, which have been shown to reduce cholesterol and the risk of heart disease. While this specific dish may not be an American classic yet, salmon sure is, and it's a wonderful ingredient to include as a staple in your diet. Its rich flavor, ease of use, and availability make it a perfect three-times-a-week feature. Dijon mustard, citrus, and spinach are some of my favorite flavors for salmon. You can cook this in minutes under a broiler or on a grill.
Serves 4

1. Preheat the broiler on low. Line a baking sheet with foil; spray it with cooking spray and set it aside.

2. In a small bowl, mix the onion with the mustard. Add the orange segments and toss to combine thoroughly. Season the mixture generously with salt and pepper.

3. Lay the salmon on the prepared baking sheet; season it with salt and pepper. Divide the onion mixture among the 4 fillets, spreading it out to cover the surface of the fish completely.

4. Broil the salmon until the onion mixture is almost charred and the salmon is just cooked through, about 8 minutes.

5. Meanwhile, heat a large nonstick sauté pan over medium-high heat. When the pan is hot, spray it with cooking spray. Add the garlic and cook, stirring, until it is very fragrant and just beginning to brown, about 1 minute. Then add the bacon bits and spinach, and season lightly with salt and pepper. Cover the pan and cook, stirring occasionally, until the spinach wilts, about 3 minutes.

6. When the spinach is cooked, remove it from the pan, draining off as much liquid as possible, and arrange it on a serving platter. Place the salmon fillets on top of the spinach, and serve.

NOW YOU CAN EAT THIS!

	Before	After
Fat	21.8g	**8.3 g**
Calories	467	**242**

Protein: 27 g | Carbohydrates: 10 g
Cholesterol: 65 mg | Fiber: 3 g
Sodium: 849 mg

RED SNAPPER FRANÇAISE WITH BUTTER AND LEMON SAUCE

4 skinless red snapper fillets (4 ounces each)

Salt and freshly ground black pepper

½ cup plus 2 tablespoons whole-wheat flour

1 cup egg substitute

Nonstick cooking spray

2 tablespoons unsalted butter

⅓ cup fresh lemon juice

⅔ cup low-fat, low-sodium chicken broth

¼ cup chopped fresh flat-leaf parsley

What makes *Française* ("in the French style") different from other sautéed dishes is the eggs. Anything cooked *à la Française* is dredged in flour first, then dipped in beaten eggs before you sauté it. Most similarly prepared dishes are dredged in flour only. The eggs add a lot of flavor and texture—but also fat. I tried using a low-fat egg substitute, and it worked like a charm. Matter of fact, enough calories were shaved off that I was able to put some butter back in and still keep it under 240 calories per serving. Now that's what I'm talking about! **Serves 4**

1. Season the fish with salt and pepper. Put the ½ cup flour in a shallow dish. Put the egg substitute in another shallow dish. Dredge the fillets in the flour, shaking off any excess. Then coat the fillets in the egg substitute and let them sit in the substitute until ready to add to the pan.

2. Heat 2 large nonstick sauté pans over medium heat. When the pans are hot, spray them with cooking spray and add 2 fillets to each pan. Cook until the fillets are golden brown and just cooked through, about 2 minutes per side. Transfer the fish to a serving platter, and tent it with foil to keep them warm.

3. In one of the sauté pans, melt the butter over high heat. Whisk the remaining 2 tablespoons flour into the butter. Add the lemon juice and chicken broth, and bring the sauce to a boil. Reduce the heat to low and simmer, whisking constantly, until the sauce thickens, about 2 minutes.

4. Stir in the parsley, and season the sauce with salt and pepper to taste, if desired. Spoon the sauce over the fish, and serve.

NOW YOU CAN EAT THIS!

	Before	After
Fat	36g	**8.6 g**
Calories	611	**232**

Protein: 29 g | Carbohydrates: 11 g
Cholesterol: 57 mg | Fiber: 2 g
Sodium: 396 mg

NOW EAT THIS! FISH AND SHELLFISH

FILLET OF
SOLE MEUNIÈRE

Meunière is fancy French for a brown butter sauce. So why would I take on a dish whose deliciousness is dependent on butter—the enemy of healthy people? Well, because first of all, it's not—the enemy, that is. The key to good taste and good health is moderation, which, as we know, is the key to many good things. Second, because I love a challenge—and because I know you'll love the result. **Serves 4**

½ cup whole-wheat flour

4 sole fillets (4 ounces each)

Salt and freshly ground black pepper

Nonstick cooking spray

12 ounces baby spinach

3 tablespoons butter

1½ tablespoons cornstarch

⅓ cup fresh lemon juice

1 cup low-fat, low-sodium chicken broth

⅓ cup chopped fresh flat-leaf parsley

1. Put the flour in a shallow dish. Season the fish with salt to taste. Dredge the fillets lightly in the flour, shaking off any excess.

2. Heat 2 large nonstick sauté pans over medium heat. When the pans are hot, spray them generously with cooking spray, and add 2 fillets to each pan. Cook until the fish is golden brown and just cooked through, about 2 minutes per side. Transfer the fish to a serving platter; tent it with foil to keep the fish warm.

3. Raise the heat under the sauté pans to high. Add the spinach to one sauté pan, and wipe the other one out with a paper towel. Season the spinach with salt, and cook, stirring often, until the spinach has wilted, about 3 minutes. Spoon the spinach next to the sole on the platter.

4. While the spinach is cooking, when the other pan is very hot, add the butter to it. Cook the butter, swirling the pan occasionally, until it is has browned and smells nutty, about 3 minutes.

5. While the butter is browning, place the cornstarch in a small bowl, and whisk in the lemon juice and chicken broth. When the butter is ready, whisk the chicken broth mixture into the pan. Simmer the sauce, stirring constantly, until it has thickened, about 2 minutes.

6. Season the sauce with salt and pepper to taste; stir in the parsley. Pour the sauce over the fish, and serve.

NOW YOU CAN **EAT THIS!**

	Before	After
Fat	44.8g	**10.7 g**
Calories	640	**259**

Protein: 26 g | Carbohydrates: 16 g
Cholesterol: 78 mg | Fiber: 4 g
Sodium: 512 mg

SEARED TUNA WITH GREEN BEANS, LEMON, AND WASABI

This dish isn't a makeover, per se. But there are so many beloved—and believe it or not, unhealthy—seared tuna dishes out there in the restaurant world that I thought I should offer at least one healthy version. The tuna is never the problem. Tuna is rich in nutrients, low in fat, delicious, and just a good bet all around. It's the stuff that's put on top that's the problem—anything from seared foie gras to deep-fried tempura crispies. Sure, it tastes great, but those additions turn a healthful dish into an artery-clogging one. **Serves 4**

1. Bring a large pot of salted water to a boil. Preheat a grill or grill pan over high heat.

2. Season the tuna steaks with salt and pepper to taste, and spray them lightly with cooking spray. When the grill is hot, add the tuna and cook for 1½ minutes per side for medium-rare. Transfer the tuna to a platter and allow it to rest, uncovered, for 5 minutes.

3. Meanwhile, cook the haricots verts in the boiling water until they are just tender, about 3 minutes; drain.

4. In a medium bowl, whisk together the lemon juice and zest, garlic, and wasabi paste. Add the haricots verts, scallions, and sesame seeds. Toss to coat, adding salt and pepper to taste.

5. Thinly slice the tuna. Fan each portion onto each of 4 plates. Pile a mound of dressed haricots verts on top of the tuna, and serve.

4 sushi-grade tuna steaks (3 ounces each)

Salt and freshly ground black pepper

Nonstick cooking spray

12 ounces haricots verts or slim green beans, trimmed

Juice and grated zest of 1 lemon

1 garlic clove, minced

2 tablespoons wasabi paste

4 scallions (white and green parts), sliced thin on the diagonal

3 tablespoons black sesame seeds

NOW YOU CAN EAT THIS!

	Before	After
Fat	43g	**3.8 g**
Calories	590	**166**

Protein: 23 g | Carbohydrates: 11 g
Cholesterol: 38 mg | Fiber: 5 g
Sodium: 211 mg

GRILLED TUNA WITH SEAWEED SALAD

2 teaspoons chili garlic sauce

4 sushi-grade tuna steaks
(4 ounces each)

Salt and freshly ground black
pepper

1½ cups seaweed salad

1½ cups sliced grape
tomatoes

4 scallions (white and green
parts), sliced thin on the
diagonal

4 tablespoons *furikake* mix

1 tablespoon toasted
sesame oil

1 tablespoon water

Even a dish as simple as grilled tuna can get out of hand if the sauces and sides are calorically wacky. In this recipe, most of the minimal fat comes from the tuna—and the rest is from toasted sesame oil, which provides a lot of flavor. The ingredient that I really love here is the *furikake,* a Japanese rice seasoning made with bonito flakes, nori flakes, and other seasonings like sesame seeds, dried anchovies, or bits of egg—the sky is the limit. It can be found, along with prepared seaweed salad, at most Asian markets.
Serves 4

1. Heat a grill or grill pan over high heat.

2. Rub the chili garlic paste into the tuna, and season the tuna with salt and pepper to taste. Grill the tuna for 2 minutes per side for rare. Transfer it to a plate, and allow it to rest for a few minutes.

3. Meanwhile, in a medium bowl, toss together the seaweed salad, tomatoes, scallions, 3 tablespoons of the *furikake,* sesame oil, and water. Divide the salad among 4 dinner plates or shallow bowls.

4. Thinly slice the tuna, and arrange the slices on top of the seaweed salad. Sprinkle the remaining *furikake* over the tuna, and serve.

NOW YOU CAN **EAT THIS!**

	Before	After
Fat	22g	**7.5 g**
Calories	491	**228**

Protein: 29 g | Carbohydrates: 10 g
Cholesterol: 51 mg | Fiber: 7 g
Sodium: 366 mg

BOUILLABAISSE

Bouillabaisse is a rich, traditional seafood stew from the south of France. It always contains garlic, saffron, and, of course, seafood. It's almost always served with a garlic-and-mayonnaise concoction called *rouille* spread on grilled bread. In order to save time, this version calls for prepared clam juice, mussels, and boneless fish fillets (in the traditional version, usually several types of small flavorful fish are sautéed in olive oil and simmered for some time). The clam juice and mussels are very flavorful. In order to save on fat and calories, there's no added olive oil—and I omitted the *rouille* and grilled bread altogether. This version is quite delicious as is and goes together quickly, so it's fine for a weeknight meal. **Serves 4**

1. In a large sauté pan over high heat, bring the fennel, garlic, white wine, saffron, sea clam juice, and marinara sauce to a boil. Reduce the heat to low, cover, and simmer until the fennel is tender, about 7 minutes.

2. Season the fish with salt and pepper to taste. Add the fish and mussels to the pan. Raise the heat to high, cover, and simmer until the fish is just cooked through and the mussels have opened, about 8 minutes.

3. Season with salt and pepper to taste, ladle into bowls, and serve.

1 fennel bulb, trimmed, cored, and sliced thin

4 garlic cloves, minced

½ cup dry white wine

1 teaspoon saffron threads

1¼ cups bottled sea clam juice

2 cups Rocco's How Low Can You Go Low-Fat Marinara Sauce (page 206) or store-bought low-fat marinara sauce

12 ounces firm white fish (such as wild striped bass or red snapper), cut into 1-inch chunks

Salt and freshly ground black pepper

1 pound mussels, beards removed, shells scrubbed and rinsed

Healthy Tips

Garlic is an awesome flavor enhancer, and virtually calorie-free. To save time, buy peeled garlic cloves and store them in water in the refrigerator to avoid oxidization.

NOW YOU CAN **EAT THIS!**

	Before	After
Fat	27 g	**3.7 g**
Calories	904	**226**

Protein: 25 g | Carbohydrates: 17 g
Cholesterol: 49 mg | Fiber: 3 g
Sodium: 968 mg

JAMBALAYA

Nonstick cooking spray

1 medium yellow onion, cut into small dice

5 garlic cloves, chopped fine

1 medium green bell pepper, seeded and cut into small dice

1 cup low-fat, low-sodium chicken broth

1 tablespoon smoked paprika

¾ cup long-grain brown rice

Salt

4 ounces andouille sausage, cut into ¼-inch-thick slices

One 14.5-ounce can diced fire-roasted tomatoes with their juices, such as Hunt's

12 ounces large shrimp, peeled and deveined, sliced in half crosswise

This Cajun dish is so associated with good times that Hank Williams named a song after it. The original isn't so good for you, though. I made a few changes to the classic to make it easier to prepare—and much healthier. White rice has been replaced with brown, and much less fat is used to cook the vegetables and meat. Feel free to improvise by adding chicken, fish, or vegetables. **Serves 4**

1. Heat a Dutch oven over medium heat. When the pot is hot, spray it with cooking spray and add the onion, garlic, and bell pepper. Sauté the vegetables, stirring occasionally, until they are almost tender, about 4 minutes. Then add the chicken broth, smoked paprika, and rice. Season to taste with salt. Cover and bring the mixture to a simmer. Reduce the heat to low, and cook for about 25 minutes.

2. Stir in the sausage and tomatoes. Cover, and continue to simmer until the rice is tender, about 30 minutes.

3. Season the shrimp with salt, and stir it into the rice mixture. Cover, and continue to cook until the shrimp is cooked through and the liquid has been absorbed, about 10 minutes.

4. Remove the pot from the heat, and let the jambalaya rest for 5 minutes. Then fluff the rice with a fork, and serve.

NOW YOU CAN **EAT THIS!**

	Before	After
Fat	34g	**10.1g**
Calories	636	**340**

Protein: 23 g | Carbohydrates: 39 g
Cholesterol: 128 mg | Fiber: 4 g
Sodium: 843 mg

BACON-WRAPPED SHRIMP AND GRITS

Grits, butter, and cheese have a highly symbiotic relationship. Similar to polenta, grits are simply ground dried corn that is rehydrated and reheated with milk, water, or broth and flavored with cheese, butter, salt, and pepper—and sometimes some other very good things. While I've been known to serve grits with black truffles, the traditional additions can pile up the fat and calories fast. Using low-fat cheese and extra-lean turkey bacon and omitting the butter reduced the fat grams from 46.7 to 7.4 and cut the calories by half. **Serves 4**

1. Wrap each shrimp with a piece of the turkey bacon, securing the bacon with a toothpick.

2. Heat a large cast-iron skillet over medium heat. When the skillet is hot, spray it generously with cooking spray. Add the prepared shrimp and cook until the bacon is crisp and the shrimp are cooked through, about 3 minutes per side.

3. Meanwhile, bring the milk, peas, and scallions to a boil in a medium saucepan over high heat. Whisk in the grits and reduce the heat to low. Cook, whisking constantly, until the grits are tender, about 5 minutes. Then whisk in the cheese, and season with salt and pepper to taste.

4. Divide the grits evenly among 4 dinner plates. Remove the toothpicks from the shrimp, place 3 shrimp on top of each plate of warm grits, and serve.

12 jumbo shrimp (about 12 ounces), peeled and deveined

6 slices extra-lean turkey bacon, cut in half

Nonstick cooking spray

1 cup skim milk

⅓ cup frozen peas

1 scallion (white and green parts), sliced thin on the diagonal

¼ cup quick-cooking grits

3 slices 2% reduced-fat cheddar singles, such as Kraft

Salt and freshly ground black pepper

NOW YOU CAN EAT THIS!

	Before	After
Fat	46.7 g	**7.4 g**
Calories	587	**231**

Protein: 24 g | Carbohydrates: 15 g
Cholesterol: 139 mg | Fiber: 1 g
Sodium: 827 mg

SHRIMP PAD THAI

4 ounces brown rice noodles

12 ounces medium shrimp, peeled and deveined

3 cups bean sprouts

8 ounces sugar snap peas, strings removed

⅜ cup Rockin' Asian Stir-Fry Sauce (page 210) or store-bought sugar-free teriyaki sauce, such as Seal Sama

2 tablespoons reduced-fat peanut butter

2 tablespoons fresh lime juice

2 tablespoons fish sauce

4 scallions (white and green parts), sliced thin on the diagonal

½ cup chopped fresh cilantro

If you've never had real pad Thai, it will change your life when you do. It's a perfect example of Asian kitchen alchemy. The texture of the rice noodles against the sweet, salty, sour, and bitter taste of the almost seventeen ingredients (in the original) is the thesis for every Asian fusion dish to come out of an American chef's kitchen since the 1980s. "Complex," "layered," and "dynamic" are words that come to mind—and every bite is different. All that comes with a price, though! The original can tip the scales at 2,000 calories per serving. This made-over version comes in at a fraction of the calories and a fraction of the work, and it tastes great. Fish sauce is derived from fermented fish and can be found in many Southeast Asian dishes. It is available in the ethnic or Asian aisle of most major supermarkets.

Serves 4

1. Bring a large pot of water to a boil, and cook the noodles according to the package directions. During the last 2 minutes of cooking, add the shrimp, 2 cups of the bean sprouts, and the sugar snap peas. Stir to distribute the ingredients evenly, and continue to cook until the vegetables are tender and the shrimp are cooked through, about 2 minutes. Drain in a colander and set aside.

2. While the shrimp are cooking, heat the teriyaki sauce in a medium saucepan over high heat. When sauce comes to a boil, whisk in the peanut butter, lime juice, fish sauce, and scallions until the mixture is smooth. Pour the sauce into a large bowl.

3. Add the cooked noodle mixture and the cilantro to the sauce, and toss until everything is completely coated. Top with the remaining 1 cup bean sprouts, and serve.

NOW YOU CAN EAT THIS!

	Before	After
Fat	45g	5.5 g
Calories	2,090	291

Protein: 26 g | Carbohydrates: 35 g
Cholesterol: 129 mg | Fiber: 4 g
Sodium: 1,363 mg

SHRIMP AND CHORIZO PAELLA

This brown-rice version of the national dish of Spain may raise some eyebrows in Barcelona, but at less than half the calories of the original, this combination of fragrant saffron, garlic, chorizo, and shrimp is a beautiful thing. **Serves 4**

1. Heat a Dutch oven over medium heat. When the pot is hot, add the chorizo and cook until the fat begins to render, about 2 minutes. Add the garlic and sauté, stirring often, until it is fragrant, about 1 minute. Then add the saffron, rice, and broth. Cover the pot and bring to a boil. Reduce the heat and cook at a very gentle simmer for about 30 minutes.

2. Stir in the diced tomatoes with their juices. Cover the pot, and continue to cook for another 25 minutes.

3. Season the shrimp with salt and pepper to taste, and stir the shrimp and frozen peas into the mixture. Cover, and continue to cook until the shrimp are cooked through and the rice is tender, about 10 minutes.

4. Allow paella to rest for about 5 minutes, covered. Then fluff the rice with a fork, and serve.

2 ounces Spanish chorizo, such as Goya, halved lengthwise and sliced into about ¼-inch-thick half-moons

6 garlic cloves, chopped

1 teaspoon saffron threads

1 cup long-grain brown rice

1¾ cups low-fat, low-sodium chicken broth

One 14.5-ounce can diced tomatoes in juice

8 ounces medium shrimp, peeled and deveined

Salt and freshly ground black pepper

¾ cup frozen peas

NOW YOU CAN **EAT THIS!**

	Before	After
Fat	42g	**8.2 g**
Calories	900	**341**

Protein: 20 g | Carbohydrates: 47 g
Cholesterol: 185 mg | Fiber: 5 g
Sodium: 883 mg

SHRIMP SCAMPI WITH BROCCOLI

6 cups large broccoli spears

2 tablespoons extra-virgin olive oil

Salt and freshly ground black pepper

1 pound large shrimp, peeled and deveined

8 garlic cloves, minced

1 tablespoon cornstarch

⅜ cup (6 tablespoons) fresh lemon juice

1½ cups low-fat, low-sodium chicken broth

1 tablespoon chopped fresh oregano

When I was young, I worked at a resort in the Poconos on the weekends. The way they made Shrimp Scampi was to simply let peeled shrimp sit in very large vat of warm garlic butter until an order came up. After many years of high-end cooking, I realized that wasn't such a bad method after all—unless you were interested in living past the age of fifty. In this version, quick-broiled shrimp and broccoli, in a butter-free lemony, garlicky sauce spiked with fresh oregano, is every bit as good. **Serves 4**

1. Preheat the oven to 450°F. Line a baking sheet with foil.

2. Lay the broccoli in a single layer on the prepared baking sheet. Drizzle ½ tablespoon of the olive oil over the broccoli, and season it generously with salt and pepper. Roast the broccoli until it starts to become tender, about 6 minutes.

3. Meanwhile, season the shrimp with salt and pepper to taste.

4. Remove the baking sheet from the oven. Turn the broiler on high. Scatter the shrimp on top of the broccoli. Broil until the shrimp are just cooked through and the broccoli is tender and beginning to brown, 5 to 6 minutes.

5. While the shrimp are cooking, heat the remaining 1½ tablespoons olive oil in a medium nonstick sauté pan over medium heat. Sauté the garlic in the hot oil until fragrant, about 2 minutes.

6. Meanwhile, place the cornstarch in a medium bowl, and whisk in the lemon juice and chicken broth.

7. Whisk the cornstarch mixture into the garlic and bring to a simmer. Add the oregano and continue to cook the sauce, whisking constantly, until it has thickened, about 1 minute. Season with salt and pepper to taste.

8. Arrange the shrimp and broccoli on a serving platter. Spoon the sauce generously over them, and serve.

NOW YOU CAN **EAT THIS!**

	Before	After
Fat	100g	**8.8 g**
Calories	1,500	**225**

Protein: 23 g | Carbohydrates: 16 g
Cholesterol: 129 mg | Fiber: 4 g
Sodium: 513 mg

JUMBO UN-FRIED SHRIMP

"Jumbo" and "shrimp" aside, there's another oxymoron at work in this recipe. How about a basket of hot, crispy fried shrimp and tartar sauce—and no eater's remorse? The key to the crispy coating is a short blast in a hot oven, not a dunking in a tub of hot oil. A word to the wise: Lobster is really delicious with this preparation, too.

Serves 4

½ cup whole-wheat flour

2 cups whole-wheat panko breadcrumbs, such as Ian's All-Natural

3 large egg whites

12 ounces jumbo shrimp, peeled and deveined

Salt and freshly ground black pepper

Nonstick cooking spray

½ cup Tartar Sauce (page 217) or store-bought low-fat tartar sauce

1. Preheat the oven to 450°F. Place a wire rack on a foil-lined baking sheet.

2. Put the flour in a shallow dish. Put the panko in another shallow dish. In a large bowl, whip the egg whites with a whisk until they are very foamy but not quite holding peaks. Working in batches, dredge the shrimp in the flour, shaking off any excess. Add the shrimp to the egg whites and toss gently to completely coat them. Working with a few at a time, add the shrimp to the panko and coat completely.

3. Lay the shrimp on the wire rack. Season them generously with salt and pepper, and spray them lightly with cooking spray.

4. Bake until the breading is golden and crispy and the shrimp are cooked through, about 8 minutes. Serve with the tartar sauce.

NOW YOU CAN **EAT THIS!**

	Before	After
Fat	17 g	**4 g**
Calories	423	**266**

Protein: 24 g | Carbohydrates: 34 g
Cholesterol: 113 mg | Fiber: 4 g
Sodium: 625 mg

SHRIMP AND ASPARAGUS STIR-FRY

1 tablespoon toasted sesame oil

1 medium Vidalia onion, sliced thin

1 large bunch asparagus, trimmed and cut on the diagonal into 1-inch pieces

1 pound large shrimp, peeled and deveined

Salt and freshly ground black pepper

⅔ cup Rockin' Asian Stir-Fry Sauce (page 210) or store-bought sugar-free teriyaki sauce, such as Seal Sama

½ cup chopped fresh basil

There are plenty of Asian stir-fry dishes that contain shrimp. Shrimp with Garlic Sauce and Creaky Shrimp were always my favorites. Don't ask what "creaky" means—I still don't know. I do know that Six Happiness Chinese Restaurant in my neighborhood in New York City was happy to deliver it within fifteen minutes, guaranteed every time. They also delivered a cardboard container—full of sugar and fat at about 800 calories a pop. This is a wholesome 600-fewer-calorie version of that "creaky" stuff: luscious shrimp, asparagus, a simple sauce, and basil. **Serves 4**

1. Heat a large nonstick sauté pan over high heat. When the pan is hot, add the sesame oil. Add the onion and asparagus, and stir-fry until the vegetables are almost tender, about 6 minutes.

2. Season the shrimp with salt and pepper to taste, and add them to the pan. Cook for about 3 minutes, stirring often. Add the stir-fry sauce. When the shrimp are cooked through and the sauce is hot (after about 2 minutes), stir in the basil. Season with salt and pepper to taste, if desired, and serve.

NOW YOU CAN EAT THIS!

	Before	After
Fat	19.1 g	**6.4 g**
Calories	873	**198**

Protein: 21 g | Carbohydrates: 14 g
Cholesterol: 129 mg | Fiber: 3 g
Sodium: 886 mg

CHICKEN AND
TURKEY

CHICKEN CORDON BLEU

Ever since I was a kid working in catering halls to pay for college, I've been fascinated by how delicious this simple dish is. Though the original has ample amounts of oozing butter, this version doesn't have *any* butter in it at all, and it still tastes great. Pay close attention to the cooking time so the chicken doesn't dry out, and prepare the sauce 2 hours ahead of cooking time. **Serves 4**

1. In a small saucepan, whisk the evaporated milk into the cornstarch. Bring the milk mixture to a boil over high heat, whisking constantly. Reduce the heat to low and continue to cook until the mixture has thickened, about 1 minute. Then whisk the cheese into the sauce until it is melted and smooth. Whisk in the chives, and season the sauce with salt and pepper to taste.

2. Spray an ice cube tray with cooking spray, and divide the cheese sauce equally among 8 of the cube holes. Freeze the cheese sauce until it is hard, about 2 hours.

3. Preheat the oven to 450°F. Place a wire rack on a foil-lined baking sheet, and set it aside.

4. Lay the chicken cutlets on a work surface, and season them with salt and pepper to taste. Arrange the ham slices over the chicken. Place 2 frozen cheese cubes in the center of each piece of chicken. Roll up the chicken to encase the filling, and secure each package with 2 toothpicks.

5. Put the flour in a shallow dish. Place the panko in another shallow dish. In a medium bowl, whip the egg whites with a whisk until they are extremely foamy but not holding peaks. Working in batches, dredge the chicken bundles in the flour, shaking off any excess. Dip them in the egg whites to coat completely. Then dredge them in the breadcrumbs to coat completely.

6. Place the chicken bundles on the wire rack. Spray the chicken lightly with cooking spray, and season with salt and pepper to taste. Bake until the breading is golden brown and crispy outside and the cheese sauce is fully melted, 25 to 30 minutes. Serve hot.

½ cup evaporated skim milk

2 teaspoons cornstarch

½ cup shredded Swiss cheese

3 tablespoons chopped fresh chives

Salt and freshly ground black pepper

Nonstick cooking spray

4 chicken cutlets (4 ounces each), pounded very thin

3 ounces thinly sliced lean ham (from the deli counter)

⅓ cup whole-wheat flour

1½ cups whole-wheat panko breadcrumbs, such as Ian's All-Natural

4 large egg whites

NOW YOU CAN **EAT THIS!**

	Before	After
Fat	81 g	**6.6 g**
Calories	1,360	**333**

Protein: 43 g | Carbohydrates: 24 g
Cholesterol: 91 mg | Fiber: 3 g
Sodium: 497 mg

CHICKEN AND DUMPLINGS

1 tablespoon plus 1 teaspoon cornstarch

1½ cups low-fat, low-sodium chicken broth

1 cup whole milk

3 large celery stalks, sliced thin on the diagonal

1 medium yellow onion, sliced thin

Salt and freshly ground black pepper

2 cups shredded skinless breast meat from a rotisserie or roast chicken

⅔ cup Bisquick Heart Smart baking mix

⅓ cup buttermilk

¼ cup chopped fresh flat-leaf parsley

This is a southern comfort food dish that some say came straight out of the Great Depression as a way to stretch a little bit of chicken to feed a big family. Flour and fat are combined to form a dumpling (such a sweet name for such an insidious food, don't you think?) that is then is cooked in broth. In real life, those sweet little dumplings are calorie bombs that call for a healthier version—like this one. Serves 4

1. Place the cornstarch in a medium bowl, and whisk in the chicken broth and milk. Pour the mixture into a large saucepan or Dutch oven and bring it to a boil, whisking constantly. Add the celery and onion. Season with salt and pepper to taste, and return to a boil. Then reduce the heat to low, cover, and simmer, stirring occasionally, until the vegetables are just tender, about 10 minutes.

2. Stir the chicken into the vegetable mixture, and raise the heat to medium-low. Cover the pot and bring to a steady simmer.

3. Meanwhile, in a medium bowl, stir the baking mix and buttermilk together until the mixture just forms a soft dough.

4. Drop 12 spoonfuls of the dumpling mixture into the pot, spacing the dumplings out as much as possible. Cover, and simmer until the dumplings are just cooked through, about 7 minutes.

5. Sprinkle the parsley over the dumplings. Season with salt and pepper to taste, if desired. Ladle into soup bowls and serve.

NOW YOU CAN **EAT THIS!**

	Before	After
Fat	49.3g	6 g
Calories	845	269

Protein: 28 g | Carbohydrates: 24 g
Cholesterol: 66 mg | Fiber: 1 g
Sodium: 738 mg

CHICKEN ALFREDO

In Italy, pasta and meats are generally served as separate courses, but in this country, we like to combine them into a single main course. This creamy pasta pairs well with the sauteed chicken. **Serves 4**

1. Bring a large pot of salted water to a boil. Add the linguine and cook according to the package directions, about 10 minutes.

2. Meanwhile, heat 2 large nonstick sauté pans over medium heat.

3. Place the flour in a shallow dish and the egg substitute in another shallow dish. Dredge the chicken in the flour, and then coat it with the egg substitute.

4. When the pans are hot, spray them with cooking spray and add 2 chicken cutlets to each pan. Sauté until the chicken is golden brown and just cooked through, about 2 minutes per side. Transfer the cutlets to a platter, cover lightly with foil to keep them warm.

5. Wipe out one of the pans with a clean paper towel and return it to medium heat. Combine the Creamy Parmigiano-Reggiano Sauce and the peas in the pan, and bring the sauce to a simmer. When the peas are hot (after about 1 minute), add the parsley; season with salt and pepper to taste, if desired.

6. Drain the pasta well and arrange it on a serving platter. Spoon half of the sauce over the pasta and sprinkle with the cheese. Lay the chicken cutlets on top of the pasta. Spoon the remaining sauce over the top, and serve immediately.

4 ounces whole-wheat linguine

½ cup whole-wheat flour

½ cup egg substitute

4 chicken cutlets, pounded thin

Nonstick cooking spray

1 cup Creamy Parmigiano-Reggiano Sauce (page 208)

⅔ cup frozen peas

¼ cup chopped fresh flat-leaf parsley

2 tablespoons grated Parmigiano-Reggiano cheese

NOW YOU CAN **EAT THIS!**

	Before	After
Fat	75 g	**5.5 g**
Calories	1,220	**320**

Protein: 33 g | Carbohydrates: 35 g
Cholesterol: 61 mg | Fiber: 5 g
Sodium: 577 mg

GRILLED CHICKEN WITH WARM MANGO SALSA

4 boneless, skinless chicken breasts, trimmed of all fat

Nonstick cooking spray

Salt and freshly ground black pepper

1 medium red onion, cut into small dice

1 small jalapeño, stemmed, seeded, and chopped fine

1 medium tomato, cut into small dice

1 large mango, seeded and skin removed (see Healthy Tips) cut into small dice

Grated zest and juice of 2 limes

2/3 cup chopped fresh cilantro

1 small avocado, seeded, peeled, and sliced

This is a light and simple chicken dish that's perfect for a summer barbecue. Although we eat more chicken than any other animal protein in the United States, the problem with most of it is that it is insipid and tired. A fruit-based salsa like this one offers some sweetness and acidity that really sparks up this ubiquitous bird. This recipe is simply too good not to include. **Serves 4**

1. Preheat a grill or grill pan over high heat.

2. Spray the chicken breasts lightly with cooking spray, and season them with salt and pepper to taste. Grill the chicken until it is just cooked through, about 3 minutes per side. Transfer the chicken to a platter, and cover it with foil to keep it warm.

3. Meanwhile, heat a large nonstick sauté pan over medium-high heat. When it is hot, spray the pan with cooking spray, and add the onion. Season with salt and pepper and cook, stirring occasionally, until almost tender, 5 to 6 minutes. Add the jalapeño, tomato, and mango, and cook the salsa, stirring it occasionally, until it is just heated through, 4 to 5 minutes.

4. Add the lime zest, lime juice, and cilantro to the salsa. Season to taste with salt, if desired. Serve the chicken with the warm salsa and avocado slices on top.

NOW YOU CAN **EAT THIS!**

	Before	After
Fat	33g	**7.2 g**
Calories	590	**274**

Protein: 35 g | Carbohydrates: 20 g
Cholesterol: 82 mg | Fiber: 5 g
Sodium: 245 mg

Healthy Tips

Here's a quick and easy way to separate a mango from its skin. Using a paring knife, make a cut through the mango, sliding the knife next to the pit and along one side of the mango. Repeat on the other side of the pit, which will leave you with two large pieces. Working with one piece at a time, make crosshatch cuts through the fruit just to the peel, but not through it. Bend the peel back and carefully slide the knife between the peel and the fruit to remove the meat from the peel. Cut up any large pieces and discard the skin.

CHICKEN AND MUSHROOM "RISOTTO"

I adore risotto. It is as much fun to make and serve as it is to eat. I have spent most of my career learning how to perfect it—and much of my life eating it. There are few foods that make people moan as much as a beautifully prepared risotto does. (Remember *Seinfeld*?) Two things make it so delicious: the starch that is released from the rice during the slow and careful cooking process, and the butter and cheese we add to it. Unfortunately, for a few pleasurable moments on the lips, it's a terror for the hips, thanks to the fat and carb content. This rice-less risotto uses something called TVP, or textured vegetable protein. It's a high-fiber, high-protein soy product. It's great both raw and cooked, and it has far fewer carbs than white rice.

Serves 4

1. In a large saucepan, combine the scallions, garlic, mushrooms, 1 cup of the milk, and the chicken broth. Bring to a boil over high heat. Season lightly with salt. Stir in the textured vegetable protein. Cover, and reduce the heat to medium-low. Simmer the "risotto" until the textured vegetable protein is tender and most of the liquid has been absorbed, about 12 minutes.

2. Meanwhile, whisk the remaining ¼ cup milk into the cornstarch in a small bowl.

3. Pour the milk mixture into the saucepan, and raise the heat to high. Bring the mixture to a vigorous boil, stirring constantly with a wooden spoon. When it has thickened (after about 1 minute), stir in the cheese and chicken. Continue to cook until the chicken is hot. Season with salt and pepper to taste, if desired, and serve immediately.

1 cup sliced scallions (white and green parts)

4 garlic cloves, minced

12 ounces cremini mushrooms, sliced

1¼ cups 2% milk

1 cup low-fat, low-sodium chicken broth

Salt

¾ cup textured vegetable protein (TVP)

1 tablespoon cornstarch

½ cup grated Parmigiano-Reggiano cheese

Shredded skinless breast meat from 1 warm rotisserie or roast chicken

Freshly ground black pepper

NOW YOU CAN EAT THIS!

	Before	After
Fat	30g	**5.9 g**
Calories	620	**268**

Protein: 36 g | Carbohydrates: 18 g
Cholesterol: 58 mg | Fiber: 4 g
Sodium: 851 mg

FLASH-FRIED FINGER-LICKIN' CHICKEN

3 cups low-fat, low-sodium chicken broth

Salt

4 skinless, bone-in chicken thighs

2 quarts grapeseed oil

1½ cups whole wheat flour

1 tablespoon sweet paprika

1½ teaspoons celery salt

1 tablespoon freshly ground black pepper

1 teaspoon salt

½ teaspoon cayenne pepper

2 cups low-fat buttermilk

Flash frying is a high-heat deep-frying technique used to rapidly brown small pieces of quick-cooking food such as tiny calamari or small shrimp to avoid overcooking them before the crust browns. Flash flying requires an oil temperature of at least 400°F—which means you have to use an oil with a high smoke point, like grapeseed oil. By poaching the chicken first and then flash frying it, I was able to eliminate 20 grams of fat and at least 250 calories from traditional fried chicken. Because the chicken is already cooked, it only has to spend enough time in the hot oil to brown the crust, which means it absorbs less oil. **Serves 4**

1. Heat the chicken broth in a medium saucepot over high heat, seasoning it generously with salt. Add the chicken thighs to the pan and bring the broth to a simmer. Cover, and reduce the heat to low. Simmer gently until the chicken is tender, about 40 minutes. Remove the thighs from the liquid, pat them dry, and set them aside on a platter; cover it with foil to keep them warm.

2. While the chicken is cooking, pour the grapeseed oil into a large pot with high sides, and bring it to 400°F over high heat. Set a wire rack in a rimmed baking sheet or over several layers of paper towels (for draining the chicken). In a shallow dish, combine the flour with the paprika, celery salt, black pepper, 1 teaspoon salt, and the cayenne. Use a whisk to thoroughly combine the ingredients.

3. Combine the warm chicken thighs with the buttermilk in a large bowl, coating them completely. Dredge the thighs in the seasoned flour. Then dip the thighs in the buttermilk and dredge them in the seasoned flour once more, to double-coat the chicken. Shake off any excess flour.

4. Fry the chicken, 2 pieces at a time, in the hot oil until deep golden brown, 30 seconds to 1 minute. Drain on the wire rack, and serve immediately.

NOW YOU CAN EAT THIS!

	Before	After
Fat	30g	**10.9 g**
Calories	549	**204**

Protein: 20 g | Carbohydrates: 7 g
Cholesterol: 58 mg | Fiber: 3 g
Sodium: 1,169 mg

NOW EAT THIS! CHICKEN AND TURKEY

CREAMY CHICKEN POT PIE

One 8-ounce package sliced button mushrooms

One 10.75-ounce can condensed low-fat cream of chicken soup, such as Campbell's Healthy Request

½ cup water

1½ teaspoons fresh thyme leaves

2 cups frozen mixed vegetables

2 cups shredded skinless chicken breast meat from a rotisserie or roast chicken

¼ cup jarred cocktail onions, roughly chopped

Freshly ground black pepper

½ cup plus 2 tablespoons Bisquick Heart Smart baking mix

⅓ cup skim milk

2 tablespoons egg substitute

Comfort food like chicken pot pie may lift your spirits, but it will weigh your body down. I know—there are few things more satisfying than biting through a super-flaky, buttery crust into a creamy, savory filling of chicken and vegetables. Pie dough is essentially flour used as a vehicle for fat. The filling can also be a fat land mine if you're not careful. Eat this. It will make you feel good in every way. **Serves 4**

1. Preheat the oven to 450°F.

2. Combine the mushrooms, soup, water, and thyme in a medium saucepan, and bring to a boil over high heat. Cover, and reduce the heat to low. Simmer until the mushrooms are almost tender, about 5 minutes.

3. Add the frozen vegetables, chicken, and onions to the saucepan. Season with pepper to taste. Pour the chicken mixture into an 8×8-inch glass baking dish.

4. In a medium bowl, combine the baking mix, milk, and egg substitute. Stir to thoroughly combine. Use an offset spatula to spread the dough over the top of the chicken mixture, covering it evenly.

5. Place the baking dish on a baking sheet, and bake until the crust is golden brown and the filling is hot and bubbly, 20 to 25 minutes. Serve hot.

NOW YOU CAN **EAT THIS!**

	Before	After
Fat	48g	**5.4 g**
Calories	800	**303**

Protein: 30 g | Carbohydrates: 33 g
Cholesterol: 66 mg | Fiber: 3 g
Sodium: 652 mg

CHICKEN PICCATA

This is one of those Italian-American classics—a dish that looks and tastes as though it was born in the Old Country but that was really born in the United States. Capers are used liberally in Sicilian cooking, and a lemon-caper sauce lives up to its name, *piccata,* which some say means "piquant." Other translations say *piccata* means to add fat—which might be where all of the butter in the original sauce comes in. This recipe calls for just a dab of butter for flavor in the tangy, tart sauce. **Serves 4**

4 skinless, boneless chicken breasts (4 ounces each), pounded thin

Salt and freshly ground black pepper

½ cup plus 2 tablespoons whole-wheat flour

1 cup egg substitute

2 tablespoons unsalted butter

4 garlic cloves, minced

⅓ cup fresh lemon juice

⅔ cup water

3 tablespoons drained capers

⅓ cup chopped fresh flat-leaf parsley

1. Heat 2 large nonstick sauté pans over medium heat.

2. While pans are heating, season the chicken with salt and pepper to taste. Put the ½ cup flour in one shallow dish and the egg substitute in another shallow dish. Dredge the chicken in the flour, then in the egg substitute, to coat completely.

3. When pans are hot, add ½ tablespoon of the butter to each pan. Allow the butter to melt completely and brown slightly. Then add 2 coated chicken breasts to each pan. Sauté the chicken until it is golden brown and just cooked through, about 2 minutes per side. Transfer the chicken to a serving platter, and tent it with foil to keep the chicken warm.

4. Raise the heat under one of the sauté pans to high. Add the remaining 1 tablespoon butter to the pan and allow it to melt. Add garlic and sweat for one minute. Whisk the remaining 2 tablespoons flour into the butter. Whisk in the lemon juice and the water; bring to a boil. Reduce the heat to low and continue to cook the sauce, whisking constantly, until it has thickened, about 2 minutes. Stir in the capers and parsley. Season with salt and pepper to taste, if desired. Spoon the sauce over the chicken, and serve.

NOW YOU CAN **EAT THIS!**

	Before	After
Fat	64g	**7.4g**
Calories	1,183	**241**

Protein: 31 g | Carbohydrates: 12 g
Cholesterol: 81 mg | Fiber: 2 g
Sodium: 459 mg

JAMAICAN JERK CHICKEN WITH CAULIFLOWER AND ASPARAGUS

Jerk is a style of cooking native to the island of Jamaica that transforms ordinary chicken into a flavorful, highly aromatic eating experience. Meats are dry-rubbed with a spice mixture called jerk seasoning, then grilled. This seasoning relies principally on two elements: allspice and Scotch bonnet peppers (among the hottest peppers on earth). Typically, whole pieces of bone-in, skin-on chicken are barbecued over wood—usually over the wood of the allspice tree. The skin is omitted here—and with that goes about 80 calories per portion. **Serves 4**

½ cup jerk marinade, such as Lawry's Caribbean Jerk

2 tablespoons Jamaican jerk seasoning, such as Johnny's Jamaica Me Crazy

1 pound boneless, skinless chicken breasts, trimmed of fat

Salt and freshly ground black pepper

Nonstick cooking spray

4 scallions (white and green parts), sliced thin on the diagonal

½ bunch asparagus, trimmed and cut on the diagonal into 1-inch pieces (2 cups)

2 cups cauliflower florets (from ½ medium head cauliflower)

½ cup chopped fresh cilantro

1. In a resealable plastic freezer bag, combine the marinade and 1 tablespoon of the jerk seasoning. Add the chicken to the bag, moving it around to coat it completely. Seal the bag and marinate the chicken for at least 30 minutes at room temperature or overnight in the refrigerator.

2. Preheat a grill or grill pan over high heat.

3. Remove the chicken from the marinade, reserving the marinade. Season the chicken with salt and pepper. Grill the chicken until it is charred and just cooked through, about 4 minutes per side. Transfer the chicken to a platter; cover it with foil to keep the chicken warm.

4. While the chicken is cooking, heat a large cast-iron skillet over medium-high heat. When the skillet is hot, spray it with cooking spray, and add the scallions, asparagus, and cauliflower. Season the vegetables with salt to taste. Cover, and sauté for 2 minutes, shaking the skillet occasionally.

5. Add the reserved marinade to the vegetables. Cover, and cook, stirring occasionally, until the vegetables are tender, about 7 minutes.

6. Stir the cilantro into the vegetables. Shred the chicken, and serve it on a bed of the vegetables.

NOW YOU CAN **EAT THIS!**

	Before	After
Fat	36.8g	**1.5 g**
Calories	742.1	**205**

Protein: 29 g | Carbohydrates: 16 g
Cholesterol: 66 mg | Fiber: 3 g
Sodium: 1,444 mg

(ALMOST) GENERAL TSO'S CHICKEN

1 cup whole-wheat flour

2 cups whole-wheat panko breadcrumbs, such as Ian's All-Natural

4 large egg whites

12 ounces boneless, skinless chicken breasts, cut into 1-inch cubes

4 cups broccoli florets

¾ cup Rockin' Asian Stir-Fry Sauce (page 210) or store-bought low-calorie, low-fat Asian sauce

3 packets (10 g) Truvia, or 3 packets (3 g) Splenda

3 tablespoons rice vinegar

2 teaspoons chili garlic sauce

2 tablespoons sesame seeds, toasted

Sweet and spicy General Tso's Chicken was likely invented in the kitchens of Chinese restaurants in New York City (its first known mention was in the *New York Times* in 1977). Some say it's similar to a classic Hunanese dish the general is said to have loved—a dish that is more sour than sweet. It's usually made with battered and deep-fried chicken thighs bathed in a glossy sauce flavored with ginger, garlic, soy sauce, chiles—and lots of sugar. This chicken breast version is breaded and baked until crisp, then tossed with a reasonable version of Tso's sauce that is low in fat and contains no sugar but is still sweet. **Serves 4**

1. Preheat the oven to 450°F. Place a wire rack on a foil-lined baking sheet, and set it aside.

2. Put the flour in a shallow dish. Put the panko in another shallow dish. In a medium bowl, whip the egg whites with a whisk until they are extremely foamy but not quite holding peaks. Working in batches, dredge the chicken in the flour, shaking off any excess. Add the chicken to the egg whites and toss to coat completely. Then add the chicken, a few pieces at a time, to the panko and toss to coat completely.

3. Spread the chicken out on the wire rack. Bake until the breading is golden and crispy and the chicken is cooked through, about 10 minutes.

4. Meanwhile, place the broccoli florets in a microwave-safe dish, and cover it with plastic wrap. Cook on high until tender, about 4 minutes. Keep the broccoli covered until ready to serve.

5. In a large bowl, combine the Rockin' Asian Stir-Fry Sauce, Truvia, rice vinegar, and chili garlic sauce. Add the cooked chicken to the bowl, and toss gently until the chicken is evenly coated with the sauce.

6. Sprinkle the sesame seeds over the chicken, and serve with the steamed broccoli.

NOW YOU CAN **EAT THIS!**

	Before	After
Fat	40.6g	**5.6 g**
Calories	843	**310**

Protein: 31 g | Carbohydrates: 33 g
Cholesterol: 49 mg | Fiber: 5 g
Sodium: 1,018 mg

CHICKEN CACCIATORE

4 boneless, skinless chicken thighs (about 4 ounces each)

Salt and freshly ground black pepper

½ tablespoon extra-virgin olive oil

One 8-ounce package sliced button mushrooms

1 large green bell pepper, seeded and cut into large dice

½ cup dry red wine

1¾ cups Rocco's How Low Can You Go Low-Fat Marinara Sauce (page 206) or store-bought low-fat marinara sauce

½ cup fresh basil, roughly chopped

Many cooks overload Italian-American-style red sauce with olive oil. While it is a healthy fat, it's still a fat. At 120 calories per tablespoon, that's a lot of leeway in the hands of a liberal cook. In this version, the olive oil has been reduced to ½ tablespoon for all 4 portions and it still tastes great. If you use chicken thighs, you'll end up with a little more cholesterol but a lot more flavor. (If your diet requires very small amounts of cholesterol, use boneless, skinless chicken breast instead of the chicken thighs, and simmer them for only 10 to 12 minutes to prevent their drying out. **Serves 4**

1. Heat a Dutch oven over medium heat. Season the chicken with salt and pepper to taste. When the pot is hot, add the olive oil. Add the chicken and sear it on both sides until it is golden brown, about 4 minutes. Transfer the chicken to a plate and set it aside.

2. Add the mushrooms and bell peppers to the Dutch oven. Season the vegetables with salt and pepper, and cook until they have softened a little bit, about 8 minutes.

3. Add the wine and cook until it has reduced by half. Add the marinara sauce and the basil, and bring the sauce to a simmer. Add the browned chicken, pushing each piece down in order to submerge it as much as possible in the sauce. Cover the pot and bring the stew to a simmer. Then reduce the heat to medium-low and simmer, covered, until the chicken is cooked through and tender, about 15 minutes. Season with salt and pepper to taste, if desired, and serve.

NOW YOU CAN **EAT THIS!**

	Before	After
Fat	38.1 g	**6.9 g**
Calories	670	**240**

Protein: 26 g | Carbohydrates: 12 g
Cholesterol: 95 mg | Fiber: 2 g
Sodium: 348 mg

REAL CHICKEN MARSALA

Classic Chicken Marsala calls for Marsala wine (of course), a fortified wine from Sicily, white flour, and butter. In this modified Chicken Marsala, the white flour and the butter had to go, but the rest was retained—especially its namesake. The combination of mushrooms, garlic, herbs, and chicken broth is as delicious as the butter-laden original. **Serves 4**

1. Heat two 12-inch nonstick skillets over medium-low heat. While the pans are heating, season the chicken with salt. Put the ½ cup flour in a shallow dish and the egg substitute in a separate shallow dish. Dredge the chicken in the flour, then in the egg substitute, to coat completely.

2. When pans are hot, spray both of them generously with olive oil spray. Add 2 chicken cutlets to each pan. Cook until golden brown on each side, about 4 minutes total. Transfer the cutlets to a serving platter, and cover it lightly with foil to keep them warm.

3. Wipe the pans out with paper towels. Raise the heat to high and return the pans to the stove. Spray both pans with olive oil spray. When the pans are hot, add 1 package of mushrooms to each pan. Cook without stirring for 3 minutes to allow the mushrooms to brown.

4. When the mushrooms are light golden, combine them in one pan. Add the garlic, and season with salt to taste. Reduce the heat to medium and cook the mushrooms for another minute, or until the garlic is fragrant.

5. Stir the remaining 1½ tablespoons flour into the mushrooms. Stir in the wine and chicken broth, and bring the sauce to a simmer. Simmer until it has the consistency of gravy, about 3 minutes.

6. Remove the pan from the heat. Stir in the yogurt, and season with salt and pepper to taste, if desired. Spoon the mushroom mixture over the chicken, and serve.

4 chicken cutlets (4 ounces each), pounded thin

Salt

½ cup plus 1½ tablespoons whole-wheat flour

½ cup egg substitute

Nonstick olive oil cooking spray

Two 8-ounce packages sliced button mushrooms

4 garlic cloves, minced

½ cup dry Marsala wine

1 cup low-fat, low-sodium chicken broth

⅓ cup Greek yogurt

Freshly ground black pepper

NOW YOU CAN **EAT THIS!**

	Before	After
Fat	37 g	**4 g**
Calories	770	**243**

Protein: 34 g | Carbohydrates: 12 g
Cholesterol: 72 mg | Fiber: 2 g
Sodium: 411 mg

GRILLED CHICKEN PARMIGIANO

Chicken Parm is one of my all-time favorite dishes. It's as much an American classic as a burger and fries or angel food cake. The good news is that Parmigiano-Reggiano cheese is made from skim milk to start with, so there is no need to replace it with "cheese food" or anything else that's unsuccessfully impersonating the real thing. In this version, thin chicken cutlets are grilled and topped with reduced-fat mozzarella and then sprinkled with breadcrumbs just before finishing the dish for a crispy browned topping. **Serves 4**

1. Preheat the oven to 400°F. Lightly spray a 9×13-inch glass baking dish with olive oil spray, and set it aside.

2. Heat a grill or grill pan over high heat. Season the chicken with salt and pepper to taste. When the grill is hot, spray the chicken lightly with olive oil spray. Grill until just cooked through, about 1½ minutes per side.

3. Spread a little less than half of the marinara sauce over the bottom of the prepared baking dish. Lay the grilled chicken breasts on top of the sauce. Spoon the remaining marinara sauce over the chicken; scatter the chopped tomatoes over the top. Sprinkle with ½ cup of the chopped basil, the mozzarella, and the Parmigiano-Reggiano.

4. Bake the chicken until the cheese has melted and is beginning to brown, 10 to 12 minutes. Sprinkle the panko and remaining basil on top, and serve.

Nonstick olive oil cooking spray

4 boneless, skinless chicken breasts (4 ounces each), trimmed of all fat, pounded thin

Salt and freshly ground black pepper

2 cups Rocco's How Low Can You Go Low-Fat Marinara Sauce (page 206) or store-bought low-fat marinara sauce

1 cup drained canned whole plum tomatoes, roughly chopped

1 cup roughly chopped fresh basil leaves

1 cup shredded reduced-fat mozzarella cheese, such as Weight Watchers

1½ ounces (about 6 table-spoons) grated Parmigiano-Reggiano cheese

½ cup whole-wheat panko breadcrumbs, such as Ian's All-Natural

NOW YOU CAN **EAT THIS!**

	Before	After
Fat	49g	**9.3 g**
Calories	1,090	**332**

Protein: 39 g | Carbohydrates: 20 g
Cholesterol: 91 mg | Fiber: 3 g
Sodium: 767 mg

ROASTED CHICKEN BURRITOS WITH CORN AND BLACK BEANS

Four 9-inch low-carb tortillas, such as La Tortilla Factory

2 cups shredded skinless breast meat from a rotisserie or roast chicken

2/3 cup canned black beans, rinsed and drained

1 cup corn salsa, such as Salpica Corn and Black Bean Salsa

1/3 cup chopped fresh cilantro

1 cup shredded romaine lettuce

3 ounces (3/4 cup) 75% reduced-fat cheddar cheese, such as Cabot, shredded

1/2 cup 2% Greek yogurt

Although white rice is always included in the fast-food version of this dish, I left it out here. It would have added about 100 calories per serving, and these burritos are really good without it—even better, I think. If you can't find corn salsa, buy fresh refrigerated salsa and stir in some low-sodium canned corn. **Serves 4**

1. Using flameproof tongs, char the tortillas briefly on each side over an open flame, or toast them under a preheated broiler. Keep the tortillas warm by covering them with a kitchen towel.

2. In a medium microwave-safe bowl, combine the shredded chicken, black beans, and salsa. Cover the bowl with plastic wrap and microwave on high until the mixture is hot throughout, about 3 minutes. Stir in the cilantro.

3. Lay the tortillas on a work surface. Spoon one fourth of the chicken mixture over the bottom third of each tortilla. Top the chicken with the lettuce, cheese, and yogurt. Fold the sides of the tortillas in over the filling, and roll the tortillas up tightly to encase the filling. Serve immediately.

NOW YOU CAN EAT THIS!

	Before	After
Fat	38g	**6.8 g**
Calories	790	**280**

Protein: 38 g | Carbohydrates: 33 g
Cholesterol: 53 mg | Fiber: 17 g
Sodium: 1,328 mg

Healthy Tips

Add all-natural plain Greek yogurt to any sauce (at the end of the cooking time, off the heat, to prevent curdling) to make the sauce richer without adding much fat. Greek yogurt is also an excellent source of protein and calcium.

SUPER-LIGHT MEXICAN CHILI CON CARNE WITH BEANS

There is much debate over whether chili should have beans in it. Some folks think beans make chili cheap—in the same way, they say, that breadcrumbs do to meatloaf. Actually, in both cases, those interloping ingredients contribute substantially to the dish. Breadcrumbs make meatloaf tender, while beans add texture and additional meatiness to chili—and lots of fiber and antioxidants, too. **Serves 4**

4 garlic cloves, minced

1 medium yellow onion, cut into fine dice

1 green bell pepper, seeded and cut into fine dice

One 35-ounce canned whole plum tomatoes, roughly chopped, juices reserved

3 tablespoons chili powder

2 tablespoons ground cumin

Salt and freshly ground black pepper

12 ounces ground turkey breast

One 14-ounce can black beans, drained

1 cup shredded 75% reduced-fat cheddar cheese, such as Cabot

1. In a Dutch oven, combine the garlic, onion, bell pepper, tomatoes and their juices, chili powder, and cumin. Bring to a boil over high heat. Season with salt and pepper to taste. Reduce the heat to low, cover, and simmer until the vegetables are tender, about 8 minutes.

2. Raise the heat to high and add the ground turkey, stirring to break it up. Add the black beans and season with salt and pepper to taste. Cover, and bring to a boil. Then reduce the heat to medium-low and simmer, stirring occasionally, until turkey is cooked through, about 8 minutes.

3. Serve the chili in bowls, with the cheese sprinkled on top.

NOW YOU CAN **EAT THIS!**

	Before	After
Fat	46g	**4.6 g**
Calories	977	**287**

Protein: 36 g | Carbohydrates: 32 g
Cholesterol: 51 mg | Fiber: 10 g
Sodium: 1,189 mg

CHEESY TURKEY ENCHILADAS WITH TOMATILLO SALSA AND CILANTRO

12 ounces ground turkey breast

Four 9-inch low-carb tortillas, such as La Tortilla Factory

⅔ cup fat-free spicy black bean dip, such as Desert Pepper Trading Company

Salt and freshly ground black pepper

One 12-ounce jar tomatillo salsa, such as Ortega

1 cup reduced-fat Mexican cheese blend, such as Weight Watchers

½ cup chopped fresh cilantro

In this country, dishes of Mexican origin have a reputation for being fat-laden and bad for you. At the same time, we can't seem to get enough of them! The funny thing is that in Mexico, the traditional food is generally fresh, healthy, and wholesome—lots of grilled fish and meats, intensely flavored (and cream-free) sauces, fresh vegetables and fruits, and herbs. The problem is the blanket of full-fat cheese and sour cream under which most Mexican-American dishes are served. The Mexican flavors we love come from healthy foods like bright-tasting tomatillos and cilantro, so I banked on them in this new version of enchiladas. **Serves 4**

1. Preheat the oven to 450°F.

2. Heat a large nonstick sauté pan over medium-high heat. Add the ground turkey and cook, stirring to break it up a little, until it is just cooked through, about 4 minutes.

3. Meanwhile, using flameproof tongs, char the tortillas lightly on each side over an open flame, or toast them under a preheated broiler. Keep the tortillas warm by covering them with a clean kitchen towel as you go.

4. Stir the black bean dip into the turkey. Season with salt and pepper to taste.

5. Lay the tortillas on a work surface, and divide the turkey mixture among them. Fold the sides of the tortillas in over the filling and roll the tortillas up tightly to encase the filling. Lay them side-by-side in a 9×13-inch baking dish.

6. Spoon the salsa over the tortillas, and sprinkle with the cheese. Bake until the cheese is bubbly and the enchiladas are hot throughout, 10 to 12 minutes.

7. Sprinkle the cilantro over the enchiladas, and serve.

NOW YOU CAN **EAT THIS!**

	Before	After
Fat	33g	**9.9 g**
Calories	990	**314**

Protein: 38 g | Carbohydrates: 32 g
Cholesterol: 59 mg | Fiber: 18 g
Sodium: 1,382 mg

GRILLED TURKEY KEBABS À LA KING

This was originally a rich chicken dish made with lots of cream and sherry, peas, and pimientos, and served on hot buttered toast points or in pastry shells. There are as many stories about its origin as there are versions of the recipe. It likely made its debut at the Brighton Beach Hotel in New York at the turn of the 19th century, created by the chef in honor of the owner, Mr. E. Clark King II. I went with a green-pepper version and added celery seeds to the sauce because that's how I like my à la king. If you can't live without the pimientos, feel free to add them—they will have virtually no impact on the fat and calorie content. **Serves 4**

1. Heat a grill or grill pan over high heat. Skewer the turkey cubes and bell pepper on 4 metal skewers, and season the turkey with salt and pepper to taste. When the grill is hot, spray the skewers with cooking spray. Grill the kebabs, turning them occasionally, until the turkey is light golden brown and just cooked through, about 20 minutes. Transfer the kebabs to a serving platter, and cover it with foil to keep them warm.

2. While the turkey is cooking, heat a small saucepan over medium heat. When the saucepan is hot, spray it with cooking spray. Add the onion and sauté until almost translucent, about 4 minutes.

3. Meanwhile, whisk the chicken broth into the cornstarch in a small bowl.

4. Whisk the broth mixture into the onion. Stirring constantly, bring the broth to a boil. Add the celery seeds and peas, return the sauce to a simmer, and cook until it has thickened, about 4 minutes.

5. Remove the sauce from the heat and stir in the yogurt. Season the sauce with salt and pepper to taste, if desired, spoon it over the kebabs, and serve.

1 pound turkey breast meat, cut into 1-inch chunks

1 large green bell pepper, seeded and cut into 1-inch pieces

Salt and freshly ground black pepper

Nonstick cooking spray

1 small yellow onion, cut into fine dice

1 cup low-fat, low-sodium chicken broth

1 tablespoon cornstarch

¼ teaspoon celery seeds

½ cup frozen peas

⅓ cup Greek yogurt

NOW YOU CAN **EAT THIS!**

	Before	After
Fat	25g	**3 g**
Calories	530	**192**

Protein: 30 g | Carbohydrates: 9 g
Cholesterol: 77 mg | Fiber: 2 g
Sodium: 397 mg

TURKEY TACOS WITH TOMATILLO SALSA

1 pound ground turkey breast

Salt and freshly ground black pepper

One 14.5-ounce can black beans, with their liquid

1 cup hot tomatillo salsa, such as Salpica Cilantro Green Olive Salsa

½ bunch scallions (white and green parts), sliced thin on the diagonal

Four 6-inch sprouted-corn tortillas, such as Ezekiel Food for Life

¾ cup store-bought fresh salsa, such as Top Crop

½ cup nonfat Greek yogurt

1½ cups shredded romaine lettuce

1 ripe avocado, pitted, peeled, and sliced

In Mexico, tacos are small, fresh, and simply prepared. I once had a *taco al pastor* there that was mind-bendingly good, and it had all of three ingredients! Somehow, when the taco got to the United States, it morphed into double-crust, Taco Bell Beef Supreme Chalupa with sour-cream-out-of-a-caulking-gun madness. Here I do my best to honor the Americanized taco everyone seems to love, while bringing some traditional flavors into the picture. **Serves 4**

1. Heat a large nonstick sauté pan over medium-high heat. Add the ground turkey to the pan, and season it with salt and pepper to taste. Cook, stirring to break up the meat, until the turkey is golden brown and cooked through, 6 minutes.

2. Add the black beans with their liquid and the tomatillo salsa. Continue to cook the mixture until it is hot throughout. Stir in the scallions.

3. Meanwhile, using flameproof tongs, char the tortillas over an open flame until each side is slightly blackened (or toast them under a preheated broiler). Keep the tortillas warm by covering them with a kitchen towel as you go.

4. Holding a warm tortilla in your hand, slightly folded, fill it with some of the turkey mixture, fresh salsa, yogurt, lettuce, and avocado. Repeat with the remaining tortillas, and serve.

NOW YOU CAN EAT THIS!

	Before	After
Fat	31.6g	**4.6 g**
Calories	571	**280**

Protein: 29 g | Carbohydrates: 35 g
Cholesterol: 41 mg | Fiber: 10 g
Sodium: 1,345 mg

TURKEY BOLOGNESE WITH NOODLES

Bolognese is a type of ragù—a thick, hearty meat sauce for pasta. As in most traditional types of ragù, this version starts with *mirepoix,* a combination of finely diced carrot, onion, and celery, to give the sauce flavor and texture. But instead of having beef as the star ingredient, this lightened-up version features ground turkey and is ladled on top of whole-grain egg noodles. **Serves 4**

1. Combine the carrot, onion, and celery in a food processor, and pulse until the vegetables are very finely chopped.

2. Heat a Dutch oven over medium-high heat. When the pan is hot, spray it with olive oil spray and add the vegetables. Cook, stirring often, until the vegetables have softened, about 5 minutes.

3. Add the turkey to the Dutch oven. Cook, stirring with a wooden spoon to break it up, until it is just cooked through, about 5 minutes.

4. Add the wine and bring the mixture to a boil. When the wine has reduced by about half, add the marinara sauce. Season with the nutmeg and salt and pepper to taste. Reduce the heat to low and simmer the sauce, stirring it occasionally, for 30 minutes.

5. Meanwhile, bring a large pot of salted water to a boil. Add the noodles and cook according to the package directions, 8 to 10 minutes; drain.

6. Divide the noodles among 4 bowls, and ladle the Bolognese sauce on top. Sprinkle each serving with 1 tablespoon of the cheese, and serve.

1 small carrot, roughly chopped

½ small yellow onion, roughly chopped

1 small celery stalk, roughly chopped

Nonstick olive oil cooking spray

12 ounces ground turkey breast

¼ cup dry red wine

2 cups Rocco's How Low Can You Go Low-Fat Marinara Sauce (page 206) or store-bought low-fat marinara sauce

Pinch of ground nutmeg

Salt and freshly ground black pepper

6 ounces medium yolk-free whole-grain noodles, such as Manischewitz

4 tablespoons grated Parmigiano-Reggiano cheese

NOW YOU CAN **EAT THIS!**

	Before	After
Fat	13g	**3.7 g**
Calories	980	**339**

Protein: 30 g | Carbohydrates: 45 g
Cholesterol: 46 mg | Fiber: 5 g
Sodium: 432 mg

GRILLED TURKEY SALISBURY STEAKS WITH TOMATOES AND PROVOLONE SAUCE

1¼ pounds ground turkey breast

3 tablespoons chopped fresh rosemary

Salt and freshly ground black pepper

Nonstick olive oil cooking spray

2 medium heirloom tomatoes, cut into ½-inch-thick slices

1 medium red onion, cut into ½-inch-thick slices

1 cup evaporated skim milk

1 tablespoon cornstarch

½ cup shredded sharp provolone cheese

Classic Salisbury steak is a patty made of ground beef and seasonings that is fried in butter or oil and smothered in a brown sauce. Although it was once considered health food by its inventor—a 19th-century English-American physician named James Salisbury—it's really not. This grilled version, made with ground turkey breast and fresh vegetables and smothered in a low-fat cheese sauce, makes the grade. **Serves 4**

1. Preheat a grill or grill pan over high heat.

2. In a medium bowl, combine the turkey and rosemary until well combined. Divide the mixture into 4 equal portions. Form each portion into an oval patty about 3 inches wide, 5 inches long, and 1 inch thick. Season the turkey "steaks" with salt and pepper to taste, and spray them lightly with olive oil spray. Place them on the hot grill.

3. Spray the tomato and onion slices with olive oil spray, and season them with salt and pepper to taste. Place them on the grill next to the turkey steaks. Grill the turkey steaks and onions for 3 to 4 minutes per side. Grill the tomato until charred and warmed through, about 2 minutes per side.

4. Meanwhile, whisk the evaporated milk into the cornstarch in a small bowl. Pour the mixture into a small saucepan, and bring it to a boil over high heat, whisking constantly. Reduce the heat to low and continue to cook until the sauce has thickened, about 1 minute. Whisk the cheese into the sauce until melted. Season the sauce with salt and pepper to taste.

5. Pile the tomato and onion slices on top of the turkey steaks. Spoon the cheese sauce on top, and serve.

NOW YOU CAN **EAT THIS!**

	Before	After
Fat	32.3g	**6 g**
Calories	440	**290**

Protein: 42 g | Carbohydrates: 15 g
Cholesterol: 83 mg | Fiber: 1 g
Sodium: 455 mg

BEEF AND
PORK

PEPPER STEAK

This dish is a prime example of how a cooking technique—in this case, charring peppers over an open flame—adds fabulous flavor to a dish without one bit of fat, sugar, carbohydrate, or salt. **Serves 4**

1. Carefully place 3 peppers on the grate of each of the 4 burners of a gas stove. Turn the heat to high and char the peppers, rotating them to cook them evenly, until the skins are mostly burnt, about 6 minutes (this can also be done under the broiler). Place the peppers in a bowl, cover it with plastic wrap, and allow the steam to build for about 7 minutes (to help steam off the skin). Using a paper towel, remove as much charred skin as possible. Pull off the stem end, including the core and seeds. Cut the peppers into ½-inch-thick rings.

2. Heat a large cast-iron skillet over medium-high heat. Season the steaks with salt and pepper. When the skillet is hot, spray it with cooking spray. Add the steaks and sauté until golden brown, about 4 minutes per side. Transfer them to a platter, and cover it with foil to keep them warm.

3. Spray the skillet with more cooking spray, and add the sliced onion. Sauté until the onion start to become tender, about 5 minutes. Add the garlic and sauté for 1 minute. Add the vinegar, scraping up any flavorful bits with a wooden spoon.

4. In a small bowl, whisk the chicken broth into the cornstarch. Whisk the cornstarch mixture into the skillet, and bring the sauce to a simmer. Stir in the marinara sauce and the evaporated milk. Return the sauce to a simmer. Add the peppers and continue to simmer for 1 minute. Stir in the chives. Season with salt and pepper to taste. Spoon the sauce over the steaks, and serve.

12 Anaheim or Cubanelle peppers (Italian frying peppers)

Four 4-ounce portions lean beef tenderloin

Salt and freshly ground black pepper

Nonstick cooking spray

1 Vidalia onion, sliced thin

5 garlic cloves, minced

3 tablespoons balsamic vinegar

1½ cups low-fat, low-sodium chicken broth

3 tablespoons cornstarch

½ cup Rocco's How Low Can You Go Low-Fat Marinara Sauce (page 206) or store-bought low-fat marinara sauce

½ cup fat-free evaporated milk

⅓ cup chopped fresh chives

NOW YOU CAN EAT THIS!

	Before	After
Fat	30g	**8.3 g**
Calories	525	**326**

Protein: 31 g | Carbohydrates: 31 g
Cholesterol: 78 mg | Fiber: 5 g
Sodium: 651 mg

HUNGARIAN BEEF GOULASH

6 garlic cloves, minced

2 large Spanish onions, cut into large dice

One 8-ounce jar roasted red peppers, drained and cut into large dice

One 28-ounce can whole plum tomatoes, roughly chopped, liquid reserved

4 cups low-fat, low-sodium chicken broth

1½ tablespoons sweet paprika

1½ tablespoons smoked paprika

1 pound beef shank, trimmed of all fat and cut into 2-inch cubes, bone discarded

Salt

½ cup Greek yogurt

Freshly ground black pepper

Goulash is a Hungarian stew made from cuts of beef that contain lots of collagen, which melts during cooking and thickens the liquid in which it's cooked. That's why this recipe calls for beef shank: it's rich and meaty but doesn't have the fat content of other cuts of beef, such as chuck. Paprika and onions are the other ingredients that give this dish its signature taste. A little yogurt to finish (instead of the traditional sour cream) provides additional richness without driving up the calorie count. **Serves 4**

1. In a Dutch oven, combine the garlic, onions, red peppers, tomatoes and their liquid, chicken broth, and sweet and smoked paprika. Bring the mixture to a boil over high heat. Then cover, reduce the heat to medium-low, and simmer until the vegetables begin to soften, about 7 minutes.

2. Season the beef cubes with salt and stir them into the stew. Cover, and simmer for about 1½ hours, stirring occasionally. The meat should be very tender.

3. Remove the pot from the heat and stir in the yogurt. Season the stew with salt and pepper to taste, and serve.

NOW YOU CAN **EAT THIS!**

	Before	After
Fat	74 g	**5.8 g**
Calories	1,306	**225**

Protein: 22 g | Carbohydrates: 24 g
Cholesterol: 36 mg | Fiber: 6 g
Sodium: 1,066 mg

BEEF STIR-FRY WITH BROCCOLI AND CAULIFLOWER

Chinese food has always been a favorite of mine—and apparently of just about everyone else in America. Even in the smallest towns, there is almost always a Chinese restaurant. The balance of sweet/sour/spicy flavors—and the fact that it's already cut up into easy-to-eat bite-size pieces—might be part of it. Making restaurant-style Chinese food healthy means getting rid of the sugar first, and then the fat. Using a large nonstick pan over high heat reduces the fat. A good low-fat, sugar-free Asian stir-fry sauce does the rest. **Serves 4**

Four 3 ounce lean filet mignon steaks, thinly sliced

Salt and freshly ground black pepper

1 tablespoon sesame oil

1 medium Vidalia onion, sliced thin

2 cups broccoli florets

2 cups cauliflower florets

¾ cup Rockin' Asian Stir-Fry Sauce (page 210) or store-bought low-fat, low-calorie Asian sauce, such as Seal Sama Teriyaki Sauce

½ cup chopped fresh cilantro

1. Heat a large nonstick sauté pan over high heat. Season the meat with salt and pepper to taste. When the pan is hot, add ½ tablespoon of the sesame oil. Add the meat and cook until it is light golden brown and still a little pink in the center, 4 minutes. Transfer the meat to a plate and tent it with foil to keep it warm.

2. In the same pan, over high heat, add the remaining ½ tablespoon sesame oil. When the oil is hot, add the onion, broccoli, and cauliflower. Stir-fry the vegetables until they are almost tender, about 6 minutes.

3. Add the Asian sauce and bring the mixture to a simmer. Add the meat and cook to warm it through. When the mixture is hot, stir in the cilantro. Season with salt and pepper to taste, if desired, and serve.

Healthy Tips

Eat more broccoli! There is more broccoli in this book than any other vegetable because of its tremendous health properties and ease of use. One cup of broccoli has only 30 calories—and so many nutrients. Eating a cup of broccoli nets your body twice the amount of vitamin C as the same amount of oranges—and almost half the calcium in the same amount of milk, with far fewer calories. An easy way to add broccoli to almost any dish is to add small-cut raw florets to the soup pot, pasta water, roasting pan, microwave dish—whatever you're cooking in—for about the last 5 minutes of cooking time.

NOW YOU CAN **EAT THIS!**

	Before	After
Fat	62g	**10.7 g**
Calories	1,024	**237**

Protein: 23 g | Carbohydrates: 13 g
Cholesterol: 57 mg | Fiber: 3 g
Sodium: 956 mg

INDIAN BEEF CURRY

Nonstick cooking spray

1 pound lean filet mignon, cut into 1-inch cubes

4 cups cauliflower florets

1 red bell pepper, seeded and cut into 1-inch pieces

4 garlic cloves, minced

1 tablespoon curry powder

1 tablespoon fish sauce

One 7-ounce container 5% Greek yogurt

1 cup fresh basil, roughly chopped

Salt and freshly ground black pepper

Few dishes are as tasty and flavorful as a good curry. Unfortunately, the amount of ghee (clarified butter) and full-fat yogurt used in a typical curry makes for a lot of XXL T-shirts. Here, lean, tender beef, intense seasoning, lots of fresh vegetables, and 5%-fat yogurt make for a skinny jeans day instead. Serves 4

1. Heat a large cast-iron pan over high heat. When pan is hot, spray it with cooking spray and add the meat. Cook, stirring once, until the meat is golden brown and medium-rare in the center, about 4 minutes. Transfer the meat to a platter and tent it with foil to keep it warm.

2. Spray the pan again with cooking spray and add the cauliflower, bell pepper, and garlic. Cover the pan and sauté the vegetables, stirring occasionally, until they are crisp-tender, about 7 minutes. Reduce the heat if necessary.

3. Add the curry powder to the pan and stir to incorporate it. Remove the pan from the heat and add the fish sauce. Return the meat to the pan. Stir in the yogurt and basil. Season with salt and pepper to taste, and serve immediately.

NOW YOU CAN EAT THIS!

	Before	After
Fat	50g	10.5 g
Calories	600	264

Protein: 32 g | Carbohydrates: 11 g
Cholesterol: 83 mg | Fiber: 4 g
Sodium: 612 mg

BEEF "STEW-FRY" WITH SHIITAKE MUSHROOMS AND BOK CHOY

1 tablespoon toasted
sesame oil

3 tablespoons chopped fresh
ginger

1 bunch scallions (white and
green parts), sliced thin on
the diagonal

3½ cups low-fat, low-sodium
chicken broth

⅓ cup reduced-sodium soy
sauce

6 ounces fresh shiitake
mushrooms, stems removed,
caps sliced thin

½ head bok choy, sliced thin

2 tablespoons rice vinegar

¼ cup low-sugar ketchup,
such as Heinz

Salt and freshly ground black
pepper

8 ounces lean beef tenderloin,
very thinly sliced

This is called a "stew-fry" because both cooking techniques are employed. There's a little bit of stir-frying, and the flavor profile is decidedly Asian, but enough liquid is added in the form of low-fat chicken broth that not a lot of oil is required, keeping things nice and light.
Serves 4

1. Heat a Dutch oven over high heat, and when the pot is hot, add the sesame oil. Add the ginger and scallions and cook until they are fragrant, about 1 minute.

2. Add the chicken broth and soy sauce, and bring the liquid to a boil. Add the shiitake mushrooms and bok choy, cover, and bring to a boil. Then reduce the heat to medium and simmer until the vegetables are tender, about 5 minutes.

3. Stir in the rice vinegar and ketchup, and season with salt and pepper if desired.

4. Remove the pot from the heat. Stir the sliced beef into the stew, allowing it to cook in the the residual heat of the liquid. Serve immediately.

Healthy Tips

For deep, rich flavor, use low-fat, low-sodium chicken broth where water is called for in savory recipes. It's great for cooking everything from beans to grains.

FILET MIGNON BÉARNAISE WITH ROASTED CAULIFLOWER

Béarnaise is one of the classic French sauces. Its standard formulation includes a lot of butter and egg yolks. In this version, I kept the licorice-tasting tarragon that's a hallmark of the sauce and let the fat and calories go. **Serves 4**

1. Preheat the oven to 450°F. Place a wire rack on a baking sheet lined with foil, and set it aside.

2. Heat a large cast-iron pan over high heat. Season the steaks with salt and pepper to taste. When the pan is hot, spray it with cooking spray and add the steaks. Sear the steaks until dark golden brown on both sides, about 2 minutes per side.

3. Transfer the steaks to the wire rack, place the baking sheet in the oven, and roast for 4 to 5 minutes for medium-rare. Remove the baking sheet from the oven, and tent it with foil to keep the steaks warm.

4. Respray the cast-iron pan generously with cooking spray, and return it to high heat. Add the cauliflower and cook, stirring occasionally, until it starts to brown, about 4 minutes. Season the cauliflower with salt and pepper to taste, transfer the pan to the oven, and roast until the cauliflower is tender, about 7 minutes.

5. Meanwhile, combine the vinegar, wine, shallots, and tarragon in a medium saucepan, and bring to a simmer over medium heat. Cook until the liquid has reduced by about half.

6. In a small bowl, whisk the chicken broth into the cornstarch. Whisk the mixture into the vinegar mixture and cook, whisking constantly, until the sauce has thickened, about 2 minutes. Remove the pan from the heat and whisk in the yogurt.

7. Season the béarnaise sauce with salt and pepper to taste, if desired. Serve the steaks and cauliflower with the sauce.

Four 4-ounce portions lean filet mignon (about 1 ½ inches thick), trimmed of all visible fat

Salt and freshly ground black pepper

Nonfat cooking spray

1 head cauliflower, cut into 1-inch florets (4 to 5 cups)

¼ cup tarragon vinegar or white wine vinegar

½ cup dry white wine

2 large shallots, chopped very fine (about ⅓ cup)

1 tablespoon dried tarragon leaves

½ cup low-fat, low-sodium chicken broth

1 ½ tablespoons cornstarch

⅔ cup Greek yogurt

NOW YOU CAN **EAT THIS!**

	Before	After
Fat	43g	**10.9 g**
Calories	700	**292**

Protein: 29 g | Carbohydrates: 13 g
Cholesterol: 85 mg | Fiber: 3 g
Sodium: 336 mg

STEAK FAJITAS WITH AVOCADO AND SALSA

Purists insist that skirt steak is the only cut of beef from which to make fajitas. Skirt steak is delicious—mostly because of the fat marbling through it. That's why this recipe calls for lean filet mignon: it has significantly less fat than skirt steak. The condiments more than make up for the flavor that fat provides. **Serves 4**

Two 6-ounce pieces lean filet mignon

Half of a 1-ounce package fajita seasoning, such as Old El Paso

Nonfat cooking spray

1 large Vidalia onion, sliced thin

1 large green bell pepper, seeded and sliced thin

½ ripe Hass avocado, peeled

1 cup store-bought fresh salsa

½ cup chopped fresh cilantro

Eight 6-inch low-carb, high-fiber tortillas, such as La Tortilla Factory

½ cup nonfat Greek yogurt

1. Heat a grill pan over high heat.

2. Season the steaks with half of the fajita seasoning, and spray them lightly with cooking spray. When the grill pan is hot, add the steaks and grill them for 3 minutes per side for medium-rare. Transfer the steaks to a platter, cover them with foil, and set them aside to rest. (Leave the grill pan on the heat.)

3. Combine the onion and pepper in a large bowl, and spray them lightly with cooking spray. Season the vegetables with the remaining fajita seasoning, and place them on the grill pan. Grill the vegetables until they are charred and crisp-tender, about 7 minutes. Transfer the vegetables to a bowl, and cover it with foil to keep them warm.

4. While the vegetables are grilling, mash the avocado lightly with a fork in a medium bowl. Stir in ¼ cup of the salsa and half of the cilantro to make the guacamole.

5. Holding them with flameproof tongs, char the tortillas on each side over an open flame. (Or toast them under the broiler.) Place the tortillas on a plate, and cover them with a towel to keep them warm.

6. Cut the steaks into thin slices.

7. To assemble the fajitas, spoon some of the guacamole onto each tortilla. Pile the steak and the pepper-onion mixture on top of the guacamole. Top with the yogurt, remaining ¾ cup salsa, and remaining ¼ cup cilantro. Serve.

NOW YOU CAN **EAT THIS!**

	Before	After
Fat	60g	**12.2 g**
Calories	1,165	**331**

Protein: 34 g | Carbohydrates: 39 g
Cholesterol: 57 mg | Fiber: 18 g
Sodium: 1,167 mg

STEAK AU POIVRE

4 tablespoons plus 1 teaspoon very coarsely ground black pepper

Four 4-ounce portions lean filet mignon (about 1 inch thick)

Salt

Nonstick cooking spray

2 tablespoons brandy or cognac

1½ cups evaporated skim milk

1½ tablespoons cornstarch

Steak au poivre (steak with peppercorns) is one of the all-time great French bistro dishes. Few things complement a great steak like peppercorns, brandy, and cream. Needless to say, the original is way out of our budget, calorically speaking. At one-fourth of the original calories and one-tenth of the fat, this version will make you wonder why it hasn't been revised until now. Serves 4

1. Heat a large cast-iron skillet over high heat.

2. Place the 4 tablespoons pepper on a small plate. Season the steaks with salt to taste, and dredge one side of each steak in the pepper, pressing down so that it adheres well.

3. When the pan is hot, spray it generously with cooking spray and add the steaks, pepper side down. Cook the steaks for 3 to 4 minutes per side for rare. Transfer the steaks to a serving platter, and tent it with foil to keep them warm.

4. Add the brandy and the remaining 1 teaspoon pepper to the skillet. While the brandy is reducing, whisk the evaporated skim milk into the cornstarch in a medium bowl.

5. When the brandy has reduced by about half, whisk the cornstarch mixture into the skillet. Bring the sauce to a boil. Then reduce the heat to low and simmer, whisking constantly, until the sauce has thickened, about 2 minutes. Spoon the sauce over the steaks, and serve.

NOW YOU CAN EAT THIS!

	Before	After
Fat	86.3g	**7.8 g**
Calories	1,325	**294**

Protein: 33 g | Carbohydrates: 18 g
Cholesterol: 80 mg | Fiber: 2 g
Sodium: 322 mg

BEEF WELLINGTON

One 1¼-pound piece lean filet mignon, trimmed of all visible fat

Salt and freshly ground black pepper

Nonstick cooking spray

1 pound button mushrooms, sliced

2 large shallots, chopped very fine (about ⅓ cup)

3 tablespoons fresh thyme, chopped

1 ounce dry sherry

1 ounce duck liver pâté

4 sheets frozen phyllo dough, thawed

This puff pastry–wrapped and pâté-packed dish is *de rigueur* for any character in a book, movie, or television show who is trying to impress someone with an über-elegant meal. The classic is rich beyond measure and fussy as hell. I've minimized its artery-clogging character—by about 77 grams of fat and 777 calories—and the fuss factor, too. It remains über-elegant. Serves 4

1. Preheat the oven to 400°F. Line a baking sheet with parchment paper, and set it aside. Place a wire baking rack on a sheet pan and set aside.

2. Heat a large cast-iron skillet over high heat. Season the meat with salt and pepper to taste. When the pan is hot, add the cooking spray. Add the meat. Sear, turning it occasionally, until the meat is a deep golden brown all over, about 4 minutes total.

3. While the meat is searing, pulse the mushrooms, in two batches, in a food processor until they are very finely chopped.

4. Remove the skillet from the heat, and transfer the meat to the wire baking rack set over the sheet pan. Spray the skillet with cooking spray and place it over medium-low heat. Add the shallots and about half of the thyme. Cook, stirring occasionally, until the shallots start to become tender and fragrant, about 2 minutes.

5. Raise the heat to high. Add the mushrooms to the skillet. Sauté, stirring occasionally, until the mushrooms have released their liquid and the liquid has mostly evaporated, about 10 minutes. Add the sherry and cook for another minute. Add the pâté and stir until it is fully incorporated into the mushrooms. Season the mixture with salt and pepper to taste. Let it cool slightly.

6. On a work surface, lay down 1 sheet of phyllo. Spray the phyllo lightly and evenly with cooking spray. Sprinkle it with one quarter of the remaining thyme. Repeat the process with the remaining 3 sheets of phyllo, stacking the sheets as you go.

7. Working with the shorter side of the phyllo toward you, spread the mushroom mixture over the lower half half of the phyllo,

	Before	After
Fat	91.3g	**11.7 g**
Calories	1,156	**335**

Protein: 38 g | Carbohydrates: 17 g
Cholesterol: 123 mg | Fiber: 2 g
Sodium: 352 mg

leaving a 1-inch border on the sides. Place the beef on top of the mushroom mixture. Fold up the sides of the phyllo on the right and left of the beef to encase it. Roll up the beef in the phyllo.

8. Place the beef-phyllo package, seam side down, on the prepared baking sheet. Spray the package lightly with cooking spray. Season it with salt and pepper.

9. Roast until the meat is medium-rare, about 20 minutes. Let the Beef Wellington rest for 5 minutes before slicing.

Healthy Tips

Phyllo dough is low in fat and contains no saturated fat or trans fats, and no cholesterol. It's light and flaky, and as long as you use butter-flavored cooking spray and/or olive oil cooking spray between layers rather than real melted butter or olive oil it's a perfect low-fat/low-calorie swap for most recipes that call for dough of any kind.

BEEF STROGANOFF

12 ounces lean filet mignon, trimmed of all visible fat, cut into 1-inch cubes

Salt and freshly ground black pepper

Nonstick cooking spray

1 large Vidalia onion, sliced thin

12 ounces white button mushrooms, sliced

1 tablespoon reduced-sugar ketchup, such as Heinz

¼ cup dry sherry

¾ cup low-fat, low-sodium beef broth

2 teaspoons cornstarch

¼ cup reduced-fat sour cream, such as Breakstone's

¼ cup chopped fresh flat-leaf parsley

There's a reason why this creamy concoction of beef, mushrooms, and onions in a sour cream sauce is a classic. What's not to like? Well, 31 grams of fat, for starters. The original has nothing on this slimmed-down version—except for about 20 grams of fat. **Serves 4**

1. Heat a large cast-iron pan over high heat. Season the beef with salt and pepper to taste. When the pan is hot, spray it with cooking spray, and add the beef. Sear the meat, turning it occasionally, until it is deep brown on the outside but still pink in the center, about 4 minutes. Transfer the meat to a plate, and tent it with foil to keep it warm.

2. Reduce the heat to medium-high and spray the pan with cooking spray. Add the onion and season with salt and pepper to taste. Cover and cook, stirring often, until the onion begins to soften, about 4 minutes. Add the mushrooms, cover, and cook until the vegetables are tender, about 6 minutes. Add the ketchup and sherry to the pan; cook until the sherry has evaporated.

3. Meanwhile, in a small bowl, whisk the broth into the cornstarch.

4. Pour the cornstarch mixture into the pan, and bring the mixture to a simmer. Cook until the sauce has thickened, about 3 minutes. Return the beef to the pan and reheat it slightly.

5. Remove the pan from the heat. Stir in the sour cream and parsley. Season with salt and pepper to taste, if desired, and serve.

NOW YOU CAN **EAT THIS!**

	Before	After
Fat	31 g	**7.2 g**
Calories	508	**222**

Protein: 23 g | Carbohydrates: 13 g
Cholesterol: 61 mg | Fiber: 2 g
Sodium: 288 mg

SHEPHERD'S PIE WITH BEEF

Swapping the traditional crown of mashed white potatoes for a topping of seasoned cauliflower puree made with Greek yogurt saves a load of calories and carbs—enough to enjoy this English pub dish with a nice pint, if you like. **Serves 4**

1. Preheat the oven to 450°F. Line a baking sheet with foil and spray it with cooking spray.

2. Lay the cauliflower on the prepared baking sheet and season it with salt and pepper to taste. Top with another sheet of foil; roll up the edges to form a tightly sealed package. Roast the cauliflower for 20 minutes. Remove the top layer of foil, being careful of the steam. Continue to roast the cauliflower until it is tender and beginning to brown, about 10 minutes. (Leave the oven on.)

3. In the bowl of a food processor, combine the cauliflower and the yogurt. Puree until smooth, about 2 minutes. Season with salt and pepper to taste, if desired. Cover to keep warm.

4. Heat a large nonstick sauté pan over medium-high heat. When the pan is hot, add the ground beef; season it with salt and pepper to taste. Cook the meat, breaking it up with a wooden spoon, until it is just cooked through, about 4 minutes. Drain the beef in a strainer; set it aside.

5. Reduce the heat under the sauté pan to medium. Add the onion to the pan and sauté until nearly tender, about 6 minutes. Add the frozen vegetables and the tomatoes. In a small bowl, whisk the chicken broth into the cornstarch. Add the cornstarch mixture to the vegetables; raise the heat to high. Bring the mixture to a simmer, stirring constantly. Then reduce the heat to medium and simmer until the sauce has thickened, about 2 minutes.

6. Add the cooked beef and the chives to the vegetable mixture. Season with salt and pepper to taste, if desired. Spread the beef mixture in an 8×8-inch glass baking dish. Spread the warm cauliflower puree over the beef mixture, and sprinkle it with the panko. Bake until the pie is hot throughout, about 8 minutes.

Nonstick cooking spray

1 medium head cauliflower, cored and cut into large florets (about 4 cups)

Salt and freshly ground black pepper

½ cup Greek yogurt

12 ounces lean ground beef

1 medium yellow onion, cut into small dice

1½ cups frozen mixed vegetables

½ cup canned diced tomatoes, drained

1 cup low-fat, low-sodium chicken broth

1 tablespoon cornstarch

3 tablespoons chopped fresh chives

⅓ cup whole-wheat panko breadcrumbs, such as Ian's All-Natural

NOW YOU CAN **EAT THIS!**

	Before	After
Fat	31 g	**11.6 g**
Calories	599	**294**

Protein: 24 g | Carbohydrates: 24 g
Cholesterol: 63 mg | Fiber: 5 g
Sodium: 508 mg

CHICKEN-FRIED STEAK WITH SAUSAGE GRAVY

This dish is emblematic of great home-style Southern cooking. Some say its origins are in Europe, where wiener schnitzel was invented—and there are some similarities. The connection ends, though, with the country-style sausage gravy with which we smother our pan-fried cutlets. Europeans serve their version with a humble (and lean) wedge of lemon. I retained the gravy but lightened it up dramatically—and instead of pan-frying the cutlets in bacon fat as they do in some parts of the South, I chose to bread and bake them. **Serves 4**

1. Preheat the oven to 450°F. Place a wire rack on a baking sheet lined with foil, and set it aside.

2. Put the flour in a shallow dish. Put the panko in another shallow dish. In a medium bowl, whip the egg whites until they are very foamy but not quite holding peaks. Dredge the steaks in the flour, shaking off any excess. Dip them in the egg whites to coat. Then dredge the steaks in the panko, coating them evenly.

3. Place the steaks on the wire rack and spray them with cooking spray. Season the steaks with salt and pepper to taste, and roast until they are golden brown and crispy, 8 to 10 minutes.

4. Meanwhile, heat a large nonstick sauté pan over high heat. When the pan is hot, add the sausage and stir it to break it up. Cook the sausage until it is just done, about 4 minutes.

5. While the sausage is cooking, whisk the chicken broth into the cornstarch in a small bowl.

6. Add the cornstarch mixture to the sausage and bring it to a simmer. When the gravy has thickened slightly (after about 2 minutes), remove the pan from the heat.

7. Stir the yogurt into the gravy. Season it with salt and pepper to taste. Pour the hot gravy over the steaks, and serve immediately.

1 cup whole-wheat flour

2 cups whole-wheat panko breadcrumbs, such as Ian's All-Natural

3 large egg whites

Four 3-ounce portions lean filet mignon, pounded about ⅓ inch thick

Nonstick cooking spray

Salt and freshly ground black pepper

One 6-ounce link hot Italian turkey sausage, casing removed

1 cup low-fat, low-sodium chicken broth

1 tablespoon cornstarch

½ cup nonfat Greek yogurt

NOW YOU CAN **EAT THIS!**

	Before	After
Fat	107 g	**10.2 g**
Calories	1,890	**317**

Protein: 32 g | Carbohydrates: 23 g
Cholesterol: 85 mg | Fiber: 3 g
Sodium: 746 mg

MEATLOAF WITH PORTOBELLO MUSHROOMS

4 ounces portobello mushrooms, roughly chopped

2 garlic cloves

⅓ cup egg substitute

⅓ cup reduced-sugar ketchup, such as Heinz

12 ounces 93% lean ground beef

¼ cup chopped fresh flat-leaf parsley

½ cup whole-wheat panko breadcrumbs, such as Ian's All-Natural

½ teaspoon salt

Freshly ground black pepper

Usually, when I make meatloaf, I just press my mother's meatball mix into a loaf pan—but that calls for pork, whole eggs, and white breadcrumbs. Not exactly spa cuisine. Instead of going for ground turkey here, I wanted to use lean beef for a richer taste. The portobello mushrooms add moistness, flavor, and bulk—in exchange for very few calories. Serves 4

1. Preheat the oven to 450°F. Line a baking sheet with foil and set it aside.

2. Place the mushrooms in a food processor, and pulse until they are very finely chopped; scrape them into a large mixing bowl. Add the garlic cloves to the food processor and pulse until they are finely chopped. Add the egg substitute and 1 tablespoon of the ketchup, and puree until the garlic is smooth. Scrape the garlic mixture into the bowl containing the mushrooms.

3. Add the beef, parsley, and panko to the bowl. Add the salt and season with pepper to taste. Using your hands, gently mix the ingredients until they are just combined.

4. On the prepared baking sheet, form the meat mixture into an 8×4×1½-inch loaf. Brush the remaining ketchup over the loaf. Bake until the meatloaf is cooked through, 18 to 20 minutes.

5. Allow the meatloaf to rest for 5 minutes before slicing.

NOW YOU CAN EAT THIS!

	Before	After
Fat	36 g	**8.9 g**
Calories	520	**212**

Protein: 21 g | Carbohydrates: 11 g
Cholesterol: 55 mg | Fiber: 2 g
Sodium: 400 mg

PORK AND SNAP PEA STIR-FRY WITH ORANGE-PEANUT SAUCE

Stir-fry is a perfect work-night dish. You cook every ingredient from start to finish in the same pan and make the sauce in the pan as well. This all happens in a matter of minutes, when you have all of your ingredients prepared ahead of time, because you are working with high heat. There aren't many home stoves that have the BTUs of a real wok in a Chinese kitchen, so use a heavy-bottomed skillet like cast iron or a stainless steel pan with a clad bottom, and get it very hot before you start. Gather your ingredients and wait until the pan is almost smoking before you begin cooking. High heat = high flavor and less need for fat. It's the original nonstick cooking technique. **Serves 4**

1. Heat a large cast iron pan over high heat. Season the pork with salt to taste. When the pan is hot, spray it with cooking spray and add the pork. Cook until the pork is light golden brown and almost cooked through, about 3 minutes. Transfer the pork to a plate, and cover with foil to keep warm.

2. Remove the pan from the heat. Spray the pan again with cooking spray and return it to the heat. Add the red bell pepper and sugar snap peas, and stir-fry until the vegetables are crisp-tender, about 4 minutes.

3. Meanwhile, combine the Asian sauce, orange juice concentrate, and peanut butter in a small bowl, and stir until the mixture is smooth.

4. Add the sauce and the cooked pork to the pan. Bring to a simmer, adding a little water if necessary to thin it. Stir in the basil and peanuts. Season with salt to taste, if desired, and serve.

1 pound lean pork loin, cut into bite-size strips

Salt and freshly ground black pepper

Nonstick cooking spray

1 red bell pepper, seeded and sliced thin

6 ounces sugar snap peas, strings removed

2/3 cup Rockin' Asian Stir-Fry Sauce (page 210) or store-bought low-fat, low-calorie teriyaki sauce, such as Seal Sama

2 tablespoons orange juice concentrate, thawed

2 tablespoons reduced-fat peanut butter

2/3 cup chopped fresh basil

2 tablespoons roasted unsalted peanuts, chopped

NOW YOU CAN EAT THIS!

	Before	After
Fat	38g	**10.9 g**
Calories	505	**297**

Protein: 31 g | Carbohydrates: 17 g
Cholesterol: 71 mg | Fiber: 3 g
Sodium: 915 mg

BARBECUE RIBS

1 rack baby back ribs (1½ to 1¾ pounds), trimmed of all visible fat

Salt and freshly ground black pepper

1 tablespoon smoked paprika

2 tablespoons liquid smoke, such as Stubb's

¾ cup reduced-sugar ketchup, such as Heinz

3 tablespoons red wine vinegar

1 large Vidalia onion, roughly chopped

12 garlic cloves, roughly chopped

I love these ribs—they're better than real BBQ for two reasons: (1) They ring in at one-third the calories and fat of the original, and (2) you can make them easily at home in your oven and enjoy BBQ even when it's raining, or too hot, or too cold, or the mosquitoes are out in droves. Serves 4

1. Preheat the oven to 425°F. Lay a 2-foot-long piece of aluminum foil on a baking sheet, and set it aside.

2. Cut the rib rack in half; season it generously with salt and pepper. Place the ribs on the prepared baking sheet.

3. In a medium bowl, combine the paprika, liquid smoke, ketchup, and red wine vinegar. Pour the sauce over the meat, turning to coat it completely. Scatter the onions and garlic over the sauce. Place another piece of foil on top, and fold up the edges of the foil to make a tightly sealed package. Roast the ribs for 30 minutes.

4. Reduce the heat to 275°F, and bake until the meat is tender, about 1 hour.

5. Slicing in between the bones, cut the ribs into 4 portions, and serve.

NOW YOU CAN EAT THIS!

	Before	After
Fat	68g	17.3 g
Calories	990	330

Protein: 28 g | Carbohydrates: 13 g
Cholesterol: 87 mg | Fiber: 2 g
Sodium: 328 mg

SMOTHERED PORK CHOPS WITH APPLES AND CHEDDAR CHEESE

Nonstick cooking spray

1 large red onion, cut into ½-inch-thick slices

3 large Granny Smith apples, peeled, cored, and cut into 6 wedges each

Salt and freshly ground black pepper

½ cup low-fat, low-sodium chicken broth

Four 4-ounce portions lean pork loin (1½ inches thick), trimmed of all visible fat

2 tablespoons coarse-grain Dijon mustard

2 tablespoons chopped fresh tarragon

½ cup shredded 50% reduced-fat cheddar cheese, such as Cabot

This recipe calls for lean boneless pork loin, and to avoid added sugar, we use fresh apples instead of applesauce. Tart Granny Smiths contribute great texture and flavor—as does a grainy Dijon mustard. Serves 4

1. Preheat the oven to 450°F. Spray a large foil-lined baking sheet with cooking spray.

2. Separate the onion rings. Lay the onion rings and apples in a single layer on the prepared baking sheet. Spray lightly with cooking spray, and season with salt and pepper to taste. Roast the apples and onions until the apples are tender and beginning to brown, about 20 minutes.

3. Turn the broiler on high. Broil the apples and onions until they are slightly charred, about 3 minutes.

4. Put about ¾ cup of the apple-onion mixture into a blender, and add the chicken broth. Puree until the mixture is smooth. (Set the remaining apples and onions aside.)

5. Heat a large cast-iron skillet over high heat. Season the pork with salt and pepper to taste. When the pan is hot, spray it with cooking spray and add the pork. Sauté until the pork is golden brown and just cooked through, about 3 minutes per side. Transfer the pork to a serving platter, and tent it with foil to keep it warm.

6. Reduce the heat under the skillet to low and add the pureed apple mixture. Whisk in the mustard. Add the remaining roasted apples and onions and the tarragon to the skillet. Remove the skillet from the heat, and season with salt and pepper to taste. Stir to evenly coat the apples and onions with the sauce.

7. Spoon the apple mixture over the pork chops, sprinkle with the cheese, and serve.

NOW YOU CAN EAT THIS!

	Before	After
Fat	15g	6.5 g
Calories	500	243

Protein: 30 g | Carbohydrates: 16 g
Cholesterol: 79 mg | Fiber: 2 g
Sodium: 526 mg

"Instead of avoiding the foods you crave, embrace them. Instead of depriving yourself, indulge in your favorite foods. Now you can, with these versions that are made to taste great with much less fat and fewer calories. Say bye-bye to guilt and hello to flavor."

PASTA AND
MORE

EGGPLANT "MANICOTTI"

Who would have thought those thin little crepes filled with ricotta and baked in red sauce and cheese could be so diabolically caloric? The fat in the ricotta, the fat in the mozzarella, the fat in the Parmigiano-Reggiano, and even the fat in the olive oil—it adds up quickly. A typical serving has about 46 grams of fat and more than 900 calories. With a few clever swaps, I got it down to just over 8 grams and 200 calories. A few meals like this, and you'll be into your little black dress in no time. **Serves 4**

1 large eggplant (about 8 inches long and 5 inches in diameter)

Salt and freshly ground black pepper

Nonstick olive oil spray

1 cup fat-free ricotta, such as Polly-O

½ cup grated Parmigiano-Reggiano cheese

½ cup chopped fresh basil

1½ cups Rocco's How Low Can You Go Low-Fat Marinara Sauce (page 206) or store-bought low-fat marinara sauce

1 cup shredded reduced-fat mozzarella cheese, such as Weight Watchers

1. Preheat the oven to 450°F. Line 2 baking sheets with parchment paper.

2. Using a large, sharp knife, square off the eggplant to make a block about 6 inches long and 4 inches wide. Slice the eggplant lengthwise into 8 slices that are about ⅙-inch thick. Lay the eggplant slices in a single layer on the prepared baking sheets. Season the eggplant with salt and pepper to taste, and spray lightly with olive oil spray. Roast until the eggplant is almost tender, about 20 minutes. Let it cool slightly. (Leave the oven on.)

3. While the eggplant is cooling, combine the ricotta, ¼ cup of the Parmigiano-Reggiano, and the basil in a medium bowl. Season the cheese mixture with salt and pepper to taste.

4. Spread ¾ cup of the marinara sauce over the bottom of a 7×10-inch baking dish.

5. Lay the roasted eggplant slices on a work surface. Spoon one eighth of the ricotta mixture onto the bottom of each piece of eggplant, and then roll it up, jelly-roll style, to encase the filling. Nestle the 8 eggplant "manicotti," seam side down, in the baking dish. Spoon the remaining ¾ cup marinara sauce over the eggplant. Sprinkle with the mozzarella and remaining ¼ cup Parmigiano-Reggiano.

6. Bake until the cheese is bubbly and the filling is hot, about 18 minutes. Serve immediately.

NOW YOU CAN **EAT THIS!**

	Before	After
Fat	46g	**8.3 g**
Calories	940	**238**

Protein: 21 g | Carbohydrates: 19 g
Cholesterol: 34 mg | Fiber: 6 g
Sodium: 754 mg

FETTUCCINE ALFREDO

8 ounces whole-wheat fettuccine

1 tablespoon butter

3 garlic cloves, minced

2 teaspoons cornstarch

Pinch of ground nutmeg

¾ cup low-fat, low-sodium chicken broth

¾ cup grated Parmigiano-Reggiano cheese

¾ cup 5% Greek yogurt

Salt and freshly ground black pepper

I once ate true Fettuccine Alfredo at Ristorante D'Alfredo in Rome, where a giant picture of its namesake owner hangs on the wall. The big flavors of the dish were brought to bear by combining outsized amounts of butter and Parmigiano-Reggiano. It was that simple: butter and cheese. Not so simple, though, if you're watching your waistline. This version eliminates the cream that many American versions call for but retains a little bit of the butter for flavor. The velvety-smooth texture is re-created with yogurt and thickened chicken broth. It may not be as authentic as the original, invented by Alfredo di Lelio, but it's a very tasty version we can all live with (for a very long time). Serves 4

1. Bring a large pot of salted water to a boil. Add the fettuccine and cook according to the package directions, 9 to 11 minutes; drain.

2. While the pasta is cooking, melt the butter in a large nonstick sauté pan over medium heat. Add the garlic and cook until it is fragrant, about 2 minutes.

3. Meanwhile, combine the cornstarch and nutmeg in a small bowl. Whisk in the chicken broth until smooth. Pour the mixture into the sauté pan, raise the heat, and bring the sauce to a simmer, whisking occasionally. Whisk in ½ cup of the cheese until it has melted. Remove the sauté pan from the heat and whisk in the yogurt until the sauce is smooth.

4. In a large bowl, toss the cooked fettuccine with the Alfredo sauce. Season with salt and pepper to taste, if desired. Top the pasta with the remaining ¼ cup cheese, and serve.

NOW YOU CAN **EAT THIS!**

	Before	After
Fat	75 g	**10.4 g**
Calories	1,220	**336**

Protein: 18 g | Carbohydrates: 47 g
Cholesterol: 27 mg | Fiber: 5 g
Sodium: 745 mg

SWEET POTATO GNOCCHI

Gnocchi are small dumplings made with cooked potatoes and just enough flour to hold them together. I swapped the traditional white potatoes for far-more-healthful sweet potatoes and paired the gnocchi with broccoli. The color combo is fabulous and so is the flavor, thanks to a sprinkling of Parmigiano-Reggiano. And while many gnocchi recipes include a cream- or butter-based sauce for tossing, these are served in a garlicky broth stirred together with a bit of Greek yogurt instead. They take a little while to make, but given the great taste and the powerhouse nutritional value of sweet potatoes—and just under 350 calories per serving—they're more than worth the trouble.

Serves 4

2 large sweet potatoes (about 1¾ pounds total)

Freshly grated nutmeg

Salt and freshly ground black pepper

About 1½ cups whole-wheat pastry flour, such as Whole Foods' 365 Everyday Value

1 cup low-fat, low-sodium chicken broth

4 garlic cloves, minced

4 cups small broccoli florets

½ cup 0% Greek yogurt

½ cup grated Parmigiano-Reggiano cheese

1. Prick the skin of the sweet potatoes with a fork and microwave them on high for 12 minutes, turning them once halfway through, until they are completely cooked. Allow the sweet potatoes to cool slightly and then scoop the flesh (there should be 1¾ cups) into a food mill or potato ricer until smooth. Dispense into a bowl and season the potato mixture with the nutmeg and salt and pepper to taste. Next, mix in the whole-wheat pastry flour ½ cup at a time until a soft, pliable but not tough dough is formed. You will probably use about 1 cup of flour.

2. Fill a pastry bag fitted with a large plain tip with the gnocchi dough (alternately, cut the bottom ¼-inch off the corner of a resealable plastic bag and fill with the sweet potato mixture. Invert a nonstick baking sheet so that the bottom is facing up. Pipe lines of the dough, about ¾ inch to 1 inch thick, directly onto the baking sheet. Space the dough lines at least 1 inch apart. Once you have piped all of the dough, place the sheet in the freezer and freeze the dough until it is firm, up to 30 minutes.

3. Use a chef's knife to cut through the dough at 1 inch intervals to make the gnocchi. Roll the frozen gnocchi in a little of the whole-wheat flour and transfer them to another baking sheet that has been sprinkled with some whole-wheat flour. Wrap the gnocchi with plastic wrap. Refrigerate the gnocchi for one day or freeze in a sealed plastic bag for up to two weeks.

(continued on next page)

(continued on next page)

NOW YOU CAN **EAT THIS!**

	Before	After
Fat	58g	**4.0 g**
Calories	1,030	**348**

Protein: 17 g | Carbohydrates: 65 g
Cholesterol: 9 mg | Fiber: 11 g
Sodium: 562 mg

4. Bring a very large pot of salted water to a boil.

5. Meanwhile, in a large skillet, bring the broth and garlic to a boil over high heat. Add the broccoli to the skillet. Season with salt and pepper to taste, cover, and cook until tender, about 3 minutes.

6. When the water comes to a rolling boil, add the gnocchi and stir gently with a rubber spatula to keep them from sticking to one another. Cook the gnocchi just until they rise to the surface, 4 to 6 minutes; then drain.

7. Transfer the hot broccoli to a large bowl. Stir in the yogurt until the mixture is creamy. Add the gnocchi and the cheese to the bowl, and toss gently to coat. Season with salt and pepper to taste, if desired, and serve.

Note: If you're using sweet potatoes that come wrapped in plastic, remove the plastic before microwaving. If the potatoes are cooked in plastic, they will retain too much water and your gnocchi dough will be too soft.

ZUCCHINI AND EGGPLANT VEGETABLE LASAGNA

This is for the pasta shunners out there who still find themselves pining for a big, gooey serving of lasagna. Nothing can really replace the toothsome texture of fresh pasta, but given the amount of "bad" carbs a serving of pasta contains, it's understandable that some choose to avoid it altogether. Thin slices of zucchini and eggplant stand in for the pasta in this lasagna, made with fat-free ricotta and low-fat marinara sauce. It all adds up to a truly delish alternative to traditional high-calorie lasagna. **Serves 5**

1. Preheat the broiler on high. Line 3 baking sheets with aluminum foil and spray them with olive oil spray.

2. Lay the eggplant slices, in a single layer if possible, on one of the prepared baking sheets. Lay the mushroom slices on the second prepared baking sheet, and the zucchini slices on the third sheet. Season the vegetables with salt and pepper to taste, and spray them lightly with olive oil spray. Broil each sheet of vegetables until they are slightly browned and mostly tender, 5 to 7 minutes.

3. Preheat the oven to 450°F. Spray a 9×13-inch baking dish with olive oil spray, and set it aside.

4. In a medium bowl, combine the ricotta and half of the Parmigiano-Reggiano. Season the cheese mixture with salt and pepper to taste.

5. Spread one quarter of the marinara sauce over the bottom of the prepared baking dish. Lay the roasted zucchini on top of the sauce, covering the bottom of the dish. Spread another quarter of the sauce over the zucchini. Spread half of the ricotta mixture over the zucchini. Repeat the process with the portobello slices, another quarter of the sauce, and the remaining ricotta mixture. Top the portobellos with the eggplant slices, and spread the remaining sauce over the eggplant. Sprinkle the mozzarella and remaining Parmigiano-Reggiano over the top of the lasagna.

6. Cover the dish with foil and bake for 15 minutes. Uncover, and continue to bake until the cheese begins to brown, another 10 minutes. Let the lasagna rest for about 5 minutes before serving.

1 large eggplant, cut in half lengthwise and sliced into long, thin strips (¼-inch thick)

3 large portobello mushrooms, sliced thin

1 large zucchini, cut in half lengthwise and sliced into long, thin strips (¼-inch thick)

Salt and freshly ground black pepper

Nonstick olive oil spray

1¼ cups nonfat ricotta

¾ cup grated Parmigiano-Reggiano cheese

3 cups Rocco's How Low Can You Go Low-Fat Marinara Sauce (page 206) or store-bought low-fat marinara sauce

1 cup shredded reduced-fat mozzarella cheese, such as Weight Watchers

NOW YOU CAN **EAT THIS!**

	Before	After
Fat	59 g	**7.7 g**
Calories	1,110	**262**

Protein: 20 g | Carbohydrates: 26 g
Cholesterol: 38 mg | Fiber: 8 g
Sodium: 760 mg

INDIVIDUAL LASAGNAS

4 multigrain lasagna noodles, such as Ronzoni Healthy Harvest lasagna noodles

Nonstick cooking spray

8 ounces ground turkey breast

1½ cups Rocco's How Low Can You Go Low-Fat Marinara Sauce (page 206) or store-bought low-fat marinara sauce

1 cup fat-free ricotta

½ cup grated Parmigiano-Reggiano cheese

1 cup shredded reduced-fat mozzarella cheese, such as Weight Watchers

¾ cup roughly chopped fresh basil

Salt and freshly ground black pepper

These little lasagnas, made with fat-free ricotta and reduced-fat mozzarella, are cheesy and satisfying and totally big on flavor. Make sure the dishes (8-inch, preferably) you use are broilerproof—they go under the flame to make the cheese brown and bubbling right before serving. **Serves 4**

1. Bring a large pot of salted water to a boil. Add the lasagna noodles and cook until tender, about 18 minutes. Drain, and reserve.

2. Heat a large sauté pan over medium heat. When the pan is hot, spray it with cooking spray. Add the turkey and cook, stirring frequently, until the meat is just cooked through, 5 to 6 minutes. Stir in the marinara sauce, ricotta, Parmigiano-Reggiano, ½ cup of the mozzarella, and the basil. Fold the lasagna noodles into the sauce. Season the mixture with salt and pepper to taste.

3. Turn the broiler to high. Lightly spray four 6-inch gratin dishes with nonstick cooking spray.

4. Lay 1 noodle in each dish, folding it on top of itself. Spoon the excess sauce on top of the noodles. Top the lasagnas with the remaining ½ cup mozzarella. Place the dishes on a baking sheet, and broil until the cheese begins to brown and the lasagnas are hot throughout, 3 to 4 minutes. Serve immediately.

NOW YOU CAN EAT THIS!

	Before	After
Fat	59 g	**8.5 g**
Calories	1,110	**336**

Protein: 33 g | Carbohydrates: 28 g
Cholesterol: 67 mg | Fiber: 5 g
Sodium: 754 mg

PENNE WITH BROCCOLI RABE AND SAUSAGE

It's the combination of bitter broccoli rabe and hot sausage that makes this one of the greatest Italian-American dishes. My mother began making this when my Uncle Joe became a butcher and could provide an unlimited supply of his own handmade pork-and-fennel sausages. It's still one of my favorites of Mama's dishes. Here I use whole-wheat penne and low-fat turkey sausage—but the rest I left just like Mama's. **Serves 4**

1. Bring a large pot of lightly salted water to a boil. Add the pasta and cook according to the package directions, about 9 minutes. During the last 2 minutes of cooking, add the broccoli rabe. Stir, and continue to cook until both pasta and broccoli rabe are tender. Drain.

2. While the pasta is cooking, heat a very large nonstick pan over medium-high heat. Add the sausage and break it up with a wooden spoon. Cook until it is golden brown and just cooked through, about 5 minutes. Transfer the sausage to a colander and set it aside to drain.

3. Wipe the pan out lightly and return it to medium-low heat. Add the sliced garlic and cook until it is fragrant and just beginning to turn golden, about 1 minute. Add the crushed red pepper and the chicken broth, and bring to a simmer. Add the cooked pasta and broccoli rabe, and allow the mixture to simmer for about 1 minute to release some of the starch from the pasta and thicken the sauce. Pour the pasta mixture into a large bowl, and toss it with the cooked sausage and the cheese. Season the pasta with salt and pepper to taste, and serve.

6 ounces whole-wheat orecchiette or penne

9 cups loosely packed broccoli rabe, trimmed and cut into bite-size chunks

1½ links hot Italian turkey sausage, casings removed

8 garlic cloves, sliced very thin

½ teaspoon crushed red pepper

⅔ cup low-fat, low-sodium chicken broth

½ cup grated Parmigiano-Reggiano cheese

Salt and freshly ground black pepper

Healthy Tips

From the Department of It's Too Good to Be True, But Is: calorie-free noodles. No, I am not kidding. Shirataki noodles made from konjac flour which comes from the root of the yam-like konjac plant grown in Japan and China.

NOW YOU CAN **EAT THIS!**

	Before	After
Fat	78.8g	**9.7 g**
Calories	1,261	**314**

Protein: 23 g | Carbohydrates: 37 g
Cholesterol: 49 mg | Fiber: 6 g
Sodium: 940 mg

MACARONI AND CHEESE WITH A CRUSTY CRUNCH

Nonstick cooking spray

4 ounces whole-wheat elbow macaroni

½ cup Onion-Garlic Puree (page 213)

½ teaspoon dry mustard

Pinch of cayenne pepper

1 cup shredded 50% reduced-fat cheddar, such as Cabot

⅓ cup nonfat Greek yogurt

Salt

¼ cup whole-wheat panko breadcrumbs, such as Ian's All-Natural

¼ cup grated Parmigiano-Reggiano cheese

Of all the dishes that were suggested for this book, mac 'n' cheese came up most often. Everyone loves it—and everyone knows how nutritionally bad it can be. Calories start at 600 per serving and go into the thousands. It's a dish that has become so rich that taming its fatty side proved to be quite a challenge. The base of the sauce in this version isn't cream, but a puree of cooked onions and garlic. It gives the dish lots of flavor with not so much as a gram of fat. The very hot oven makes the breadcrumbs on top get nice and crunchy. It's the combination of crisp and gooey textures that makes this a winning dish. **Serves 4**

1. Preheat the oven to 425°F. Spray an 8×8-inch baking dish with cooking spray, and set it aside.

2. Bring a large pot of salted water to a boil. Add the macaroni and cook according to the package directions, 7 to 9 minutes; drain.

3. While the pasta is cooking, bring the Onion-Garlic Puree, mustard, and cayenne to a simmer in a small saucepan over medium heat, stirring often. Whisk in the cheddar until it has melted. Remove the pan from the heat and whisk in the yogurt.

4. In a medium bowl, toss the cooked macaroni with the cheese sauce to coat thoroughly. Season with salt to taste. Pour the macaroni into the prepared baking dish, and sprinkle the panko over the top. Top with the Parmigiano-Reggiano.

5. Bake until the cheese has melted and the macaroni is hot throughout, about 10 minutes. Serve immediately.

NOW YOU CAN **EAT THIS!**

	Before	After
Fat	32g	**6.5 g**
Calories	670	**227**

Protein: 16 g | Carbohydrates: 29 g
Cholesterol: 20 mg | Fiber: 3 g
Sodium: 487 mg

NO CREAM-NO CRY
PENNE ALLA VODKA

The dirty little secret about Penne alla Vodka is not the vodka but the hefty amount of heavy cream. Vodka is colorless, odorless, and without much flavor—not really attributes of a superstar ingredient. It's the combination of cream and tomato sauce that gives this dish its signature flavor. The traditional cream is swapped here for low-fat Greek yogurt. **Serves 4**

1. Bring a large pot of lightly salted water to a boil. Add the pasta and cook according to the package directions, about 9 minutes; drain.

2. While the pasta is cooking, bring the marinara sauce and crushed red pepper to a simmer in a large nonstick sauté pan over medium heat. Cook the sauce, stirring it occasionally with a heat-resistant rubber spatula, until it is slightly thickened, about 5 minutes. Remove the sauté pan from the heat.

3. Stir about ½ cup of the marinara sauce into the yogurt until smooth (this tempers it and prevents the yogurt from curdling). Then whisk the yogurt mixture back into the marinara sauce.

4. In a large serving bowl, toss the sauce with the drained penne and the basil. Season with salt and pepper to taste. Sprinkle the cheese on top, and serve.

8 ounces whole-wheat penne

2 cups Rocco's How Low Can You Go Low-Fat Marinara Sauce (page 206) or store-bought low-fat marinara sauce

Pinch of crushed red pepper

One 7-ounce container 2% Greek yogurt

1 cup chopped fresh basil

Salt and freshly ground black pepper

6 tablespoons grated Parmigiano-Reggiano cheese

Healthy Tips

Whole-wheat pasta has a dense texture that makes it a little tougher than regular pasta. Some people like that chewiness; some don't. If you're in the latter category, overcook it a bit. Toward the end of the cooking time, keep testing it until it's as tender as you like it.

NOW YOU CAN **EAT THIS!**

	Before	After
Fat	60g	**4.8 g**
Calories	618	**320**

Protein: 18 g | Carbohydrates: 55 g
Cholesterol: 11 mg | Fiber: 6 g
Sodium: 416 mg

MAMA-APPROVED SPAGHETTI AND MEATBALLS

1 small eggplant

2 cups Rocco's How Low Can You Go Low-Fat Marinara Sauce (page 206) or store-bought low-fat marinara sauce

2 tablespoons low-fat, low-sodium chicken broth

¼ small yellow onion

1 garlic clove

1 large egg white

12 ounces lean ground turkey breast

¼ cup chopped fresh flat-leaf parsley

6 tablespoons grated Parmigiano-Reggiano cheese

Salt and freshly ground black pepper

6 ounces whole-wheat spaghetti

Considering that this dish is the Holy Grail of Mama's cooking, I truly debated whether or not to mess with it. It took six attempts to make over this dish, but I finally figured the low-cal version out—and Mama loved it! **Serves 4**

1. Place the eggplant on the grate of a gas burner over a high flame. Char the eggplant, turning it every few minutes, until the skin is blackened and the flesh is cooked through; this should take about 12 minutes. (Alternatively, you can char the eggplant on a barbecue grill, on a grill pan, or on a baking sheet under the broiler of a gas or electric oven.) Allow the eggplant to cool slightly, and then cut it in half. Scrape out the flesh, being careful not to incorporate the blackened skin. Measure out ¼ cup of the flesh; reserve the remaining eggplant for another use.

2. Bring a large pot of salted water to a boil. Meanwhile, in a small sauce pot, heat the marinara sauce over medium heat.

3. In a blender, combine the chicken broth, onions, garlic, cooked eggplant, and egg white. Puree until the mixture is smooth. In a large bowl, combine the pureed mixture with the ground turkey, parsley, and 2 tablespoons of the cheese. Season lightly with salt and pepper. Divide the meat mixture into 8 equal portions, a little over 2 ounces each.

4. When the marinara sauce comes to a simmer, roll each portion of the meatball mixture with the palms of your hands to form a ball, and gently drop the meatballs, one by one, into the hot marinara sauce. Shake the pan gently to coat the meatballs with sauce. Cover the pan, and when the sauce begins to simmer, reduce the heat to low. Simmer the meatballs for 12 minutes. Gently turn each meatball over in the marinara sauce and simmer for another 5 minutes.

5. While the meatballs are cooking, cook the pasta in the boiling water according to the package directions, about 10 minutes; drain.

6. Divide the spaghetti among 4 plates, and top each plate of pasta with 2 meatballs and some sauce. Sprinkle the remaining 4 tablespoons cheese on top, and serve.

NOW YOU CAN EAT THIS!

	Before	After
Fat	91 g	**4.4 g**
Calories	1,500	**337**

Protein: 32 g | Carbohydrates: 43 g
Cholesterol: 49 mg | Fiber: 5 g
Sodium: 487 mg

SPAGHETTI CARBONARA

8 ounces whole-wheat spaghetti

Nonstick cooking spray

1 large yellow onion, sliced thin

Salt and freshly ground black pepper

4 garlic cloves, minced

½ cup evaporated skim milk

2 large egg yolks

⅓ cup real bacon bits, such as Hormel Real Bacon Bits

⅓ cup grated Parmigiano-Reggiano cheese

Though they are both outrageously rich pasta sauces, carbonara and Alfredo are distinctly different. The base for Alfredo is cream and Parmigiano-Reggiano. The base for carbonara includes onions, bacon or pancetta (originally it was *guanciale*—cured pigs' cheeks), egg yolks, and Parmigiano-Reggiano or Pecorino Romano. At almost 1,000 calories per serving, this dish was ripe for a makeover.
Serves 4

1. Bring a large pot of salted water to a boil. Add the pasta and cook according to the package directions, about 10 minutes. Drain.

2. While the pasta is cooking, heat a large cast-iron skillet over high heat. When the skillet is hot, spray it with cooking spray and add the sliced onion. Season the onion with salt and pepper to taste and sauté, stirring occasionally, for 6 mintues or until almost tender. Reduce the heat to medium-low and add the garlic. Continue to cook until the onion is tender, about 5 minutes.

3. Meanwhile, in a small bowl, whisk together the evaporated milk and the egg yolks.

4. Add the bacon and the pasta to the skillet containing the onions and garlic, and mix well. Remove the skillet from the heat and add the egg mixture. Toss the pasta with tongs to coat it, allowing the residual heat to thicken the sauce. Stir in the cheese, and season the pasta with salt and pepper to taste, if desired. Serve immediately.

NOW YOU CAN **EAT THIS!**

	Before	After
Fat	51.6g	**7g**
Calories	967	**331**

Protein: 19 g | Carbohydrates: 52 g
Cholesterol: 119 mg | Fiber: 5 g
Sodium: 584 mg

NOW EAT THIS! PASTA AND MORE

SHRIMP AND SESAME SOBA NOODLES WITH SCALLIONS

The Japanese spin buckwheat flour into culinary gold with their rich, flavorful soba noodles. Buckwheat flour has many health benefits, including being much richer in antioxidants than wheat pasta. If you have a choice, buy *inaka* or "country" soba, because it's made entirely from whole, unrefined buckwheat—which means more fiber. Traditionally, soba is served hot in a broth or cold with a sweetened soy dipping sauce called *tsuyu*. This simplified version is flavored with sesame, an American favorite. **Serves 4**

1. Bring a large pot of water to a boil. Add the noodles and cook according to the package directions, about 4 minutes. During the last 2 minutes of cooking, add the shrimp and snow peas to the pot and cook them with the noodles for 2 minutes; drain.

2. In a large bowl, combine the drained noodles, shrimp, and snow peas with the Asian sauce, scallions, and sesame seeds. Toss the mixture to coat the ingredients completely in the sauce, and serve immediately.

5 ounces soba noodles (Japanese buckwheat noodles)

8 ounces shrimp, peeled and deveined

6 ounces fresh snow peas, strings removed

⅔ cup Rockin' Asian Stir-Fry Sauce (page 210) or store-bought low-fat, low-calorie Asian sauce

1 bunch scallions (white and green parts), sliced thin on the diagonal

2 tablespoons sesame seeds, toasted

NOW YOU CAN **EAT THIS!**

	Before	After
Fat	16 g	**4.7 g**
Calories	570	**262**

Protein: 20 g | Carbohydrates: 37 g
Cholesterol: 86 mg | Fiber: 4 g
Sodium: 1,026 mg

SIDES

Down Home Baked Beans,
Creamed Spinach,
and Sweet Potato Puree

CREAMED SPINACH

Here's a great steakhouse side dish that can do more harm than the red meat itself. Standard preparations make a bad boy out of an otherwise extraordinarily healthy vegetable. The problem with spinach is that it's very lean and often bitter—which is why we sauté it in butter or douse it with cream. All-natural Greek yogurt has been employed here to help clean up its act. **Serves 4**

1 tablespoon unsalted butter

3 garlic cloves, minced

2 large shallots, chopped fine (about ⅓ cup)

Salt and freshly ground black pepper

Pinch of ground nutmeg

12 ounces baby spinach

1 teaspoon cornstarch

⅓ cup Greek yogurt

1. Heat a large nonstick sauté pan over medium heat. Add the butter to the pan, and when it has melted, add the garlic and shallots. Season with salt, pepper, and a pinch of nutmeg. Cook, stirring often, until the shallots are tender, about 4 minutes.

2. Raise the heat to high and add half of the spinach. Season it lightly with salt and pepper. Toss and stir the spinach as it cooks down. When there is enough room in the pan, add the remaining spinach. Continue to cook, stirring often, until the spinach is tender, about 3 minutes.

3. Sprinkle the cornstarch over the spinach and stir until combined. Continue to cook the spinach until the liquid has thickened, about 1 minute.

4. Remove the pan from the heat. Add the yogurt and stir to coat the spinach. Season with salt and pepper to taste, if desired, and serve.

NOW YOU CAN **EAT THIS!**

	Before	After
Fat	21.9g	**5.3 g**
Calories	294	**90**

Protein: 4 g | Carbohydrates: 9 g
Cholesterol: 13 mg | Fiber: 2 g
Sodium: 229 mg

DOWN HOME
BAKED BEANS

½ cup Pour-It-On Barbecue Sauce (page 209)

¼ teaspoon dry mustard

⅓ cut small white onion, grated

3 tablespoons real bacon bits, such as Hormel Real Bacon Bits

1 cup cannellini beans, drained

1 cup fresh kale, cleaned and roughly chopped

Salt and freshly ground black pepper

The beans in this dish are native to North America, but baked beans in some form are served all over the world. We most probably borrowed the recipe for this version (beans in tomato sauce) from our friends in England a couple hundred years ago. Baked beans are usually prepared with high amounts of sugar and salt, but other than that are generally good for you. By using a sugar-free, low-fat barbecue sauce as a base, there was some room in the calorie budget for low-fat bacon. If you prefer a more Southern taste, try substituting ½ cup canned, drained collard greens for the kale. **Serves 4** (see photograph on page 184)

In a small saucepan over high heat, combine the barbecue sauce with the dry mustard, onion, bacon bits, beans, and kale. Bring to a boil, reduce the heat to low, and simmer the beans for 10 minutes, or until the kale is tender, stirring occasionally. The sauce should thicken slightly and the beans should be very tender. Season the beans with salt and pepper to taste, and serve.

NOW YOU CAN **EAT THIS!**

	Before	After
Fat	3.5 g	**1.6 g**
Calories	250	**113**

Protein: 7 g | Carbohydrates: 18 g
Cholesterol: 4 mg | Fiber: 4 g
Sodium: 570 mg

Healthy Tips

Eat more kale! It has one of the highest levels of antioxidants of any vegetable and is loaded with anti-cancer phytochemicals, calcium, B vitamins, and fiber. It's easier to prepare than you might think. (Just be sure to wash it well first and to remove the fibrous center rib.) Try it raw—shredded in salads—or cooked. I like it roughly chopped and sautéed with garlic and a little olive oil, or braised in chicken broth, or even roasted: toss it with a little olive oil or toasted sesame oil, salt, and pepper, and roast in a single layer in a shallow baking pan at 500 degrees until the edges are starting to brown and turn crispy and the centers are slightly wilted.

GOOEY GARLIC CHEESE BREAD

This was a tough one. Everyone loves cheesy garlic bread, but between the white bread, the butter, and the cheese, it's a tough sell to the health-conscious. The task was to figure out how to get whole-wheat bread to respond like white bread. Toasting the bread first, then dipping it in chicken broth before topping it with a generous amount of low-fat cheese, and finally broiling it did the trick.

Serves 4

1. Preheat the oven to 450°F. Line a baking sheet with foil.

2. Split the baguette in half crosswise, then lengthwise, to make 4 pieces. Rub the entire surface of each piece of bread with the garlic. Place the bread, cut side up, on the prepared baking sheet and bake until the bread begins to brown, about 8 minutes.

3. Remove the bread from the oven. Turn the broiler on high.

4. Pour the chicken broth into a small bowl, and dunk each piece of bread in the broth, allowing it to absorb a good amount of liquid. Place the soaked pieces of baguette back on the baking sheet, cut side up. Season them with salt and crushed red pepper to taste. Sprinkle with the Parmigiano-Reggiano and mozzarella. Broil the bread until the cheese is bubbly and beginning to brown, about 3 minutes.

5. Sprinkle the parsley over the bread, cut each piece in half, and serve.

8 ounces whole-wheat baguette

2 garlic cloves

2 cups low-fat, low-sodium chicken broth

Salt

Crushed red pepper

¼ cup grated Parmigiano-Reggiano cheese

¾ cup shredded reduced-fat mozzarella, such as Weight Watchers

3 tablespoons chopped fresh flat-leaf parsley

Healthy Tips

Parsley is the world's most popular herb, and for good reason. It adds a mild, fresh flavor and an eye-catching green color. A sprig of parsley provides much more than a decoration on your plate, though. It's a good source of folic acid—one of the most important B vitamins, which help prevent heart disease.

NOW YOU CAN **EAT THIS!**

	Before	After
Fat	63 g	**6.9 g**
Calories	790	**224**

Protein: 10 g | Carbohydrates: 28 g
Cholesterol: 16 mg | Fiber: 3 g
Sodium: 740 mg

RED APPLE COLESLAW

½ cup Rocco's Magnificent Mayonnaise (page 200) or store-bought low-fat mayonnaise, such as Hellmann's Low-Fat Mayonnaise Dressing

1 tablespoon red wine vinegar

1 packet (3.5 g) Truvia

1 teaspoon celery seeds

2 cups shredded red coleslaw mix

½ bunch scallions (green and white parts), sliced thin on the diagonal

1 large sweet Red Delicious apple, grated with its skin

Salt and freshly ground black pepper

Coleslaw goes with so many things. You'll rarely see a cookout without it. The crunchy shredded raw cabbage and the sweet-and-sour flavor make it a wonderfully piquant counterpoint to the grilled meats and BBQ sauce–slathered main dishes that make up America's favorite backyard menus. **Serves 4**
(see photograph on page 191)

In a large bowl, whisk the mayonnaise, vinegar, sweetener, and celery seeds together. Add the coleslaw mix, scallions, and grated apple. Season with salt and pepper to taste. Toss to thoroughly combine the ingredients. Chill, covered, until cold, about 2 hours.

NOW YOU CAN **EAT THIS!**

	Before	After
Fat	23g	**2.5 g**
Calories	260	**78**

Protein: 2 g | Carbohydrates: 13 g
Cholesterol: 6 mg | Fiber: 2 g
Sodium: 328 mg

SIMPLE MACARONI SALAD

A deli side-dish favorite, macaroni salad is a gimme on every table in America come summertime. Everyone has a favorite recipe—some contain ham, some peppers, some bacon, and some peas. But all contain high-fat mayonnaise and white pasta, a fundamentally bad combo. White pasta is replaced here with whole-wheat shells, and the high-fat mayo with low-fat mayo. I added a few bits and pieces, like smoked paprika, to give it some personality. **Serves 4** (see photograph on page 191)

1. Bring a large pot of salted water to a boil. Add the shells and cook according to the package directions, 6 to 9 minutes; drain. Rinse the pasta in cool water. Drain again and let it cool completely.

2. Combine the mayonnaise and paprika in a large bowl. Add the cooled pasta and the carrot, celery, bell pepper, and scallions. Toss to combine. Season with salt and pepper to taste, if desired. Chill, covered, until cold, about 2 hours.

4 ounces whole-grain shells or elbow macaroni

⅔ cup Rocco's Magnificent Mayonnaise (page 200) or store-bought low-fat mayonnaise, such as Hellmann's Low-Fat Mayonnaise Dressing

1½ tablespoons smoked paprika

1 medium carrot, shredded

2 celery stalks, sliced thin on the diagonal

½ red bell pepper, cut into small dice

½ bunch scallions (white and green parts), sliced thin on the diagonal

Salt and freshly ground black pepper

NOW YOU CAN EAT THIS!

	Before	After
Fat	26 g	**3.8 g**
Calories	360	**171**

Protein: 6 g | Carbohydrates: 30 g
Cholesterol: 8 mg | Fiber: 5 g
Sodium: 258 mg

GERMAN SWEET POTATO SALAD

2 medium sweet potatoes

1½ cups cauliflower florets

2 tablespoons white wine vinegar

1 packet (3.5 g) Truvia

1 bunch scallions (white and green parts), sliced thin on the diagonal

5 tablespoons real bacon bits, such as Hormel Real Bacon Bits

⅓ cup chopped fresh flat-leaf parsley

Salt and freshly ground black pepper

There are two basic types of potato salad: mayonnaise-based and sugar-and-vinegar-based. I have always preferred the latter because of the sweet-and-sour element—plus it has bacon in it. This alluring sweet-and-sour salad replaces not-so-nice white potatoes with sweet potatoes (much nicer for you), and the texture of the salad has been bulked up with cauliflower. **Serves 4**

1. Prick the sweet potatoes with a fork, and microwave them on high just until they are tender, about 7 minutes, turning them halfway through the cooking. Let the sweet potatoes cool until they can be handled.

2. Meanwhile, place the cauliflower in a large microwave-safe dish. Cover it tightly and microwave on high until just cooked through, about 5 minutes. Let cool slightly.

3. Peel the sweet potatoes and cut them into large dice.

4. In a large bowl, whisk together the white wine vinegar and Truvia. Add the sweet potatoes, cauliflower, scallions, bacon bits, and parsley; toss to coat. Season the salad with salt and pepper to taste, and serve.

NOW YOU CAN **EAT THIS!**

	Before	After
Fat	27.4 g	**2 g**
Calories	460	**112**

Protein: 6 g | Carbohydrates: 18 g
Cholesterol: 6 mg | Fiber: 4 g
Sodium: 475 mg

German Sweet Potato Salad,
Red Apple Coleslaw,
and Simple Macaroni Salad

BETTER THAN MASHED "POTATOES"

Nonstick cooking spray

2½ cups roughly chopped cauliflower

Salt and freshly ground black pepper

½ cup Greek yogurt

Few dishes are as soul-satisfying and luxurious as a buttery-rich potato puree or mashed potatoes. I love mashed potatoes, but I know that they're not particularly good for me. Cauliflower puree makes a truly superb substitute. **Serves 4**

1. Preheat the oven to 450°F. Line a baking sheet with foil and spray it with cooking spray.

2. Spread the cauliflower out on the prepared baking sheet. Season it with salt and pepper to taste. Top the cauliflower with another sheet of foil, and roll up the edges to form a sealed package.

3. Roast the cauliflower for 20 minutes. Remove the top foil, being careful of the steam, and continue roasting the cauliflower until it is tender, another 15 to 20 minutes.

4. In the bowl of a food processor, combine the cauliflower with the yogurt. Puree until the mixture is smooth. Season with salt and pepper to taste, if desired, and serve.

NOW YOU CAN EAT THIS!

	Before	After
Fat	30g	**2.8g**
Calories	390	**48**

Protein: 2 g | Carbohydrates: 5 g
Cholesterol: 8 mg | Fiber: 2 g
Sodium: 181 mg

Healthy Tips

There may be no real replacement for a big, fat, fluffy baked potato—and once in a while, do treat yourself to one (topped with Greek yogurt and chopped fresh chives). But on a regular basis, reduce the amount of white potatoes in your diet by replacing them with cauliflower in recipes like potato salad or mashed potatoes.

SWEET POTATO PUREE

I learned that sweet potatoes are the single healthiest vegetable. They're loaded with carotenoids, vitamin C, potassium, and fiber. You can dress them up a bunch of different ways, but this simple puree is ideal. **Serves 4**
(see photograph on page 184)

2 large sweet potatoes

Salt and freshly ground black pepper

1. Prick the skin of the sweet potatoes with a fork. Place the potatoes in a microwave-safe dish and microwave on high until they are completely tender, about 13 minutes, turning them once halfway through cooking.

2. Split the sweet potatoes in half, and scoop the flesh into the bowl of a food processor. Puree the sweet potatoes until smooth. Season with salt and pepper to taste; serve warm.

NOW YOU CAN **EAT THIS!**

	Before	After
Fat	30 g	**0 g**
Calories	390	**70**

Protein: 1 g | Carbohydrates: 16 g
Cholesterol: 0 mg | Fiber: 2 g
Sodium: 190 mg

SWEET POTATO FRIES

French fries are maddeningly delicious, but consider that a large order of McDonald's French fries contains about 500 calories and 25 grams of fat *before* you dip them into ketchup or mayo. I think its time for French fry rehab, don't you? **Serves 4**

2 medium sweet potatoes, scrubbed

Salt

Nonstick cooking spray

2 tablespoons fresh thyme leaves

Freshly ground black pepper

Sweet paprika

Cayenne pepper

1. Slice the sweet potatoes lengthwise into ¼-inch-thick slices. Cut the slices into ¼-inch-wide sticks. Place the sweet potatoes in a large bowl, and sprinkle generously with salt. Let stand for about 20 minutes to release some of their moisture.

2. Meanwhile, preheat the oven to 450°F. Place a wire rack on a baking sheet, and set it aside.

3. Spread the potatoes out on paper towels to absorb any excess moisture. Then place them in a large bowl, and spray them with cooking spray. Sprinkle with the thyme and salt, pepper, paprika, and cayenne to taste. Spread the potatoes out on the prepared baking sheet.

4. Bake the fries until they are golden and tender, 35 to 45 minutes. Serve immediately.

Healthy Tips

Eat more sweet potatoes! At only 130 to 160 calories each, they are loaded with complex carbohydrates, protein, vitamins A and C, iron, and calcium—and when eaten with the skin, they have more fiber than a bowl of oatmeal.

NOW YOU CAN **EAT THIS!**

	Before	After
Fat	25g	**0.1 g**
Calories	500	**58**

Protein: 1 g | Carbohydrates: 14 g
Cholesterol: 0 mg | Fiber: 2 g
Sodium: 327 mg

LOADED BAKED POTATO SKINS

2 medium russet potatoes (about 8 ounces each), scrubbed

Nonstick cooking spray

Salt and freshly ground black pepper

1½ cups shredded 75% reduced-fat cheddar cheese, such as Cabot

¼ cup real bacon bits, such as Hormel Real Bacon Bits

¼ cup reduced-fat sour cream, such as Breakstone's

2 tablespoons chopped fresh chives

This is a healthy version of one of the greatest inventions of the 1980s: the hollowed-out deep-fried potato skins filled with sour cream, bacon, and cheese that first appeared on the menu at T.G.I. Friday's in New York City. There are a few differences, though. Here, the potato skin is baked until crisp, not fried, and the fillings are all reduced-fat products. The result is a pretty spectacular loaded potato skin at one-third of the calories and less than one-fourth of the fat of the original. **Serves 4**

1. Preheat the oven to 475°F. Line a baking sheet with foil, and set it aside.

2. Prick the surface of the potatoes several times with a fork. Microwave the potatoes on high until they are completely cooked through, about 12 minutes, turning them halfway through the cooking time. Let the potatoes cool until you can handle them. Then cut each potato in half lengthwise, and using a small spoon, scoop out and discard (or reserve for another use) the flesh of the potatoes, leaving a very thin wall of flesh on the skin, less than ¼ inch thick.

3. Place the potato shells on the prepared baking sheet. Spray them, inside and out, with cooking spray, and season with salt and pepper to taste. Bake the potato shells until they are golden brown and beginning to crisp, about 10 minutes.

4. Divide the cheese among the potato shells. Sprinkle the bacon pieces on top of the cheese, and bake until the cheese is bubbly, about 8 minutes.

5. Serve the potatoes topped with a dollop of sour cream and a sprinkling of chives.

NOW YOU CAN **EAT THIS!**

	Before	After
Fat	39.7 g	**6.6 g**
Calories	649	**187**

Protein: 18 g | Carbohydrates: 14 g
Cholesterol: 24 mg | Fiber: 2 g
Sodium: 678 mg

NOW EAT THIS! SIDES

SAUCES

ROCCO'S MAGNIFICENT MAYONNAISE

6 tablespoons white vinegar

4 tablespoons cornstarch

1 17.6-ounce container Greek yogurt

3 tablespoons Dijon mustard

4 packets (14 g) Truvia

1 teaspoon salt

Real mayonnaise is made with egg yolks and oil—which might explain the 10 grams of fat *per tablespoon.* You can very easily wind up slathering at least a tablespoon or two on a sandwich. This very good approximation uses Greek yogurt as a base, rather than oil.
Makes 2¾ cups (about 44 1-tablespoon servings)

1. In a small bowl, whisk the vinegar into the cornstarch. Whisk ⅔ cup of the yogurt into the vinegar mixture. Pour the yogurt and vinegar mixture into a small saucepan and cook over high heat, whisking constantly, until it comes to a boil. (The yogurt mixture will thicken very quickly.) When it is very thick, scrape it into the bowl of a food processor.

2. Blend the yogurt mixture for about 1 minute. Turn off the food processor and scrape down the sides of the bowl. Continue to blend the yogurt mixture until it is slightly cool and very smooth, about 3 more minutes. Add the remaining yogurt, mustard, Truvia, and salt to the mixture. Blend for another minute. Scrape down the sides of the bowl and blend for 30 more seconds.

3. Pour the mayonnaise into a plastic container. Cover tightly and place in the refrigerator until it is cold and firm, about 2 hours. The mayonnaise can be stored in the refrigerator for up to 1 week.

NOW YOU CAN **EAT THIS!**

	Before	After
Fat	10g	**1.1 g**
Calories	360	**18**

Protein: 0 g | Carbohydrates: 1 g
Cholesterol: 3 mg | Fiber: 0 g
Sodium: 85 mg

3-GRAMS-OF-FAT BLUE CHEESE DRESSING

Believe it or not, it wasn't so long ago that most people thought blue cheese was a bit exotic—a stinky, strange cheese with (heaven forbid!) mold in its veins. But blue has gained traction because its rich, creamy texture and tangy taste are fabulous—whether eaten out of hand, crumbled over a salad, or stirred into a dressing. But this is no lean cheese, my friends. Thankfully, a little goes a long way, and there are great-tasting low-fat blue cheeses available in most major supermarkets today. **Makes 2¼ cups (18 servings)**

In a large bowl, whisk together the mayonnaise, sour cream, buttermilk, lemon juice, garlic paste, Worcestershire sauce, and blue cheese. Season with salt and pepper to taste. Store in a covered container in the refrigerator for up to 3 days.

1 cup Rocco's Magnificent Mayonnaise (page 200) or store-bought low-fat mayonnaise, such as Hellmann's Low-Fat Mayonnaise Dressing

½ cup reduced-fat sour cream, such as Breakstone's

¼ cup buttermilk

1 tablespoon fresh lemon juice

1 garlic clove, mashed to a paste

1 teaspoon Worcestershire sauce

5 ounces reduced-fat blue cheese, such as Treasure Cove

Salt and freshly ground black pepper

NOW YOU CAN **EAT THIS!**

	Before	After
Fat	19g	**3.4 g**
Calories	170	**52**

Protein: 3 g | Carbohydrates: 2 g
Cholesterol: 9 mg | Fiber: 0 g
Sodium: 226 mg

NOT YOUR MAMA'S RANCH DRESSING

½ cup reduced-fat sour cream, such as Breakstone's

½ cup Rocco's Magnificent Mayonnaise (page 200) or store-bought low-fat mayonnaise, such as Hellmann's Low-Fat Mayonnaise Dressing

¾ cup buttermilk

2 garlic cloves, mashed to a paste

2 tablespoons fresh lemon juice

Freshly ground black pepper

1 tablespoon Worcestershire sauce

1 teaspoon celery salt

3 tablespoons chopped fresh chives

3 tablespoons chopped fresh flat-leaf parsley

Ranch dressing has been the top-selling dressing in this country since 1992, when it overtook Italian. Given that the bottled stuff has 19 grams of fat and 180 calories per serving, something had to be done! We may want many things like our mamas'—but not the fat-laden version of this dressing. **Makes 2 cups (about 15 servings)**

Combine all the ingredients in a medium bowl, and whisk to blend. Store covered in the refrigerator for up to 3 days.

NOW YOU CAN **EAT THIS!**

	Before	After
Fat	19 g	**1.7 g**
Calories	180	**29**

Protein: 1 g | Carbohydrates: 2 g
Cholesterol: 5 mg | Fiber: 0 g
Sodium: 130 mg

"RUSSIAN ISLAND" DRESSING

The original Russian dressing was actually made with yogurt. Early in the 20th century, some chef in Chicago replaced the yogurt with mayonnaise—and that's when it became one of the most popular salad dressings in the country. That little tweak also made it one of the most caloric and unhealthy salad dressings around. In this version, the best of both Russian *and* Thousand Island dressing, the fat has been reduced from 16 grams to less than 1 gram per serving. It's perfect for salads, charcuterie—and, of course, the classic Reuben sandwich. **Makes 1¼ cups (10 servings)**
(see photograph on page 214)

Combine all the ingredients in a medium bowl, and whisk until fully combined. Store in a covered container in the refrigerator for up to 3 days.

½ cup Rocco's Magnificent Mayonnaise (page 200) or store-bought low-fat mayonnaise, such as Hellmann's Low-Fat Mayonnaise Dressing

½ cup reduced-sugar ketchup, such as Heinz

1 dill pickle, chopped fine (about ⅓ cup)

1 garlic clove, mashed to a paste

1 tablespoon fresh lemon juice

1 packet (3.5 g) Truvia

1 teaspoon celery salt

1 teaspoon sweet paprika

1 tablespoon hot sauce, such as Frank's RedHot Original

NOW YOU CAN **EAT THIS!**

	Before	After
Fat	16g	**0.9 g**
Calories	160	**20**

Protein: 0 g | Carbohydrates: 2 g
Cholesterol: 2 mg | Fiber: 0 g
Sodium: 220 mg

NOT SO BASIC VINAIGRETTE

4 small shallots

5 tablespoons water

2 tablespoons Dijon mustard

2 tablespoons sherry vinegar

2 tablespoons fresh lemon juice

1½ tablespoons fresh flat-leaf parsley, chopped fine

2 tablespoons extra-virgin olive oil

Salt and freshly ground black pepper

I first learned how to make a real French vinaigrette when I was eighteen years old and living with a very generous chef in Paris. It was actually his twelve-year-old daughter who taught me. The first thing she did was separate two eggs and put the yolks in a bowl; these were followed by Dijon mustard, then vinegar, then olive oil—fat (egg yolk) followed by fat (olive oil). It's the Dijon–sherry vinegar combo that really makes this dressing—and those are both fat-free. A shallot puree provides the thick texture you normally get from creating an egg yolk/olive oil emulsion. Use this to dress salads and cooked vegetables—both hot and cold. **Makes ¾ cup (6 servings)**

1. Roughly chop 2 of the shallots. Place the chopped shallots and the water in a microwave-safe bowl, cover it tightly, and microwave on high until the shallots are tender, about 5 minutes.

2. Pour the cooked shallots and cooking water into a blender. Add the mustard, vinegar, and lemon juice. Blend until the mixture is very smooth; pour into a bowl. Chop the remaining 2 shallots very fine; add them to the bowl. Add the parsley and olive oil. Season generously with salt and pepper. Gently whisk the mixture to make a broken vinaigrette (one that is intentionally not emulsified).

3. Serve immediately, or store in a covered container in the refrigerator for up to 2 weeks. Bring to room temperature and whisk gently before using.

NOW YOU CAN **EAT THIS!**

	Before	After
Fat	12g	**4.5g**
Calories	120	**64**

Protein: 1 g | Carbohydrates: 4 g
Cholesterol: 0 mg | Fiber: 0 g
Sodium: 221 mg

CREAMY BASIL PESTO

Typical pesto can be more than 50 percent pure fat, and even though a little goes a long way, that's just too many calories. This is a re-invention of the classic *pesto alla genovese*. The garlic, pine nuts, basil, and Parmigiano-Reggiano are all still there, but low-fat sour cream stands in for the olive oil. It may not be 100 percent authentic, but you'll love what it does for your dress size. **Makes 1³/₄ cups (7 servings)**

Combine the garlic and sour cream in the bowl of a food proces-sor, and pulse until the garlic is finely chopped. Add the basil, parsley, crushed red pepper, cheese, and pine nuts. Puree until the sauce is smooth. Season with salt and pepper to taste. Store in a covered container in the refrigerator for up to 3 days.

4 large garlic cloves, coarsely chopped

1 cup reduced-fat sour cream, such as Breakstone's

2 cups packed fresh basil leaves

¹/₃ cup chopped fresh flat-leaf parsley

¹/₄ teaspoon crushed red pepper

¹/₂ cup grated Parmigiano-Reggiano cheese

2 tablespoons chopped toasted pine nuts

Salt and freshly ground black pepper

NOW YOU CAN **EAT THIS!**

	Before	After
Fat	28g	**8.3 g**
Calories	300	**110**

Protein: 6 g | Carbohydrates: 4 g
Cholesterol: 17 mg | Fiber: 0 g
Sodium: 197 mg

ROCCO'S HOW LOW CAN YOU GO LOW-FAT MARINARA SAUCE

½ tablespoon extra-virgin olive oil

6 garlic cloves, minced

1 large yellow onion, cut into small dice

Salt

Crushed red pepper

Two 28-ounce cans tomato puree

½ cup water

1 small piece of Parmigiano-Reggiano cheese rind

1 large sprig fresh basil

There are some high-quality, great-tasting low-fat tomato sauces available on the store shelves these days, so if you don't want to make sauce from scratch (don't tell Mama!), you'd do well with any of the leading brands. But my name is Rocco, after all, and I figured I was under obligation to include at least one from-scratch marinara sauce. There's just a hint of olive oil in it; everything else was bulked up to create great flavor. **Makes 6½ cups (13 servings)**

1. Heat a Dutch oven over medium heat. When the pot is hot, add the olive oil. Add the garlic and onion, and season them with salt and crushed red pepper to taste. Cook, stirring occasionally, until the onion and garlic are translucent, about 4 minutes.

2. Add the tomato puree, water, and Parmigiano-Reggiano rind to the pot. Bring to a simmer. Then cover, reduce the heat to low, and simmer for about 25 minutes.

3. With the back of a knife, bruise the basil and stir the sprig into the sauce. Simmer the sauce, uncovered, for 5 minutes. Season with salt and crushed red pepper to taste, if desired. Serve, or store in a covered container in the refrigerator for up to 5 days.

NOW YOU CAN EAT THIS!

	Before	After
Fat	1.5g	**0.8 g**
Calories	80	**55**

Protein: 2 g | Carbohydrates: 9 g
Cholesterol: 1 mg | Fiber: 1 g
Sodium: 137 mg

Healthy Tips

- When you must use fat, always use extra-virgin olive oil from the first cold press. It is the purest and the most intensely flavored. In subsequent pressings, heat and chemicals are applied to the olives to create maximum extraction. The process degrades the quality of the oil—which means more is required for the same flavor impact as just a little bit of first cold-pressed extra-virgin.

- Adding the rind of a piece of Parmigiano-Reggiano to the pot of marinara sauce as it simmers is a great way to add flavor without adding any measurable fat.

- And just add 1½ teaspoons crushed red pepper to the marinara sauce to make your own spicy and flavorful fra diavolo sauce.

MEAT SAUCE

The key to making this basic meat sauce taste so great is to use beef shank—a very flavorful cut—and a splash of dry red wine. The long cooking time breaks the meat down until it is meltingly tender.
Makes 4 cups (8 servings)

1. Heat a Dutch oven over high heat. Pat the meat dry with a paper towel, and season it with salt and pepper to taste. When the pan is hot, spray it with cooking spray. Add the meat to the pot and cook, stirring occasionally, until it is browned on all sides, 8 to 10 minutes. Transfer the meat to a plate, and set it aside.

2. Raise the heat to medium-low. Spray the pot with cooking spray, and add the carrot, celery, and onion. Cook, stirring often, until the vegetables begin to soften, about 4 minutes.

3. Add the wine, and cook until it has reduced by about half, about 3 minutes. Add the broth and marinara sauce. Season with salt and pepper to taste, cover, and bring to a simmer. Simmer the sauce over low heat, stirring it occasionally, until the meat is extremely tender, about 3 hours.

4. Stir the sauce to break up the meat. Season with salt and pepper to taste, if desired. Serve, or store in a covered container in the refrigerator for up to 3 days.

1 pound boneless beef shank, cut into 1-inch cubes

Salt and freshly ground black pepper

Nonstick cooking spray

1 small carrot, diced fine (about ⅓ cup)

1 small celery stalk, diced fine (about ⅓ cup)

½ small onion, diced fine (about ⅓ cup)

½ cup dry red wine

½ cup low-fat, low-sodium chicken broth

3 cups Rocco's How Low Can You Go Low-Fat Marinara Sauce (page 206) or store-bought low-fat marinara sauce

NOW YOU CAN **EAT THIS!**

	Before	After
Fat	3g	**2.3 g**
Calories	130	**128**

Protein: 14 g | Carbohydrates: 9 g
Cholesterol: 22 mg | Fiber: 1 g
Sodium: 255 mg

CREAMY PARMIGIANO-REGGIANO SAUCE

½ cup Onion-Garlic Puree (page 213)

1 cup whole milk

1 tablespoon cornstarch

½ cup grated Parmigiano-Reggiano cheese

Pinch of ground nutmeg

Salt and freshly ground black pepper

Toss this creamy sauce with hot cooked pasta, or drizzle it over steamed broccoli or roasted Brussels sprouts. **Makes 1½ cups (6 servings)**

1. Heat the Onion-Garlic Puree in a small saucepan over medium heat.

2. Meanwhile, in a small bowl, whisk the milk into the cornstarch.

3. Whisk the cornstarch mixture into the Garlic-Onion Puree. Raise the heat to high and bring the mixture to a boil, whisking constantly. Then reduce the heat to low and continue to cook the sauce until it has thickened, about 1 minute.

4. Add the cheese and the nutmeg to the sauce and whisk until melted. Season with salt and pepper to taste. Serve, or store in a covered container in the refrigerator for up to 3 days.

NOW YOU CAN **EAT THIS!**

	Before	After
Fat	35g	**3.3 g**
Calories	380	**66**

Protein: 4 g | Carbohydrates: 5 g
Cholesterol: 10 mg | Fiber: 0 g
Sodium: 265 mg

POUR-IT-ON BARBECUE SAUCE

Barbecue may be America's greatest contribution to the global culinary repertoire. We figured out how to take rich, fatty, often tough cuts of meat and smoke them into submission until they're melt-in-your-mouth tender. Then we slather them with sugar-laden, high-fat sauce. Here's a sugar-free, zero-fat BBQ sauce that packs flavor without pulling punches. **Makes 2 cups (16 servings)**

1½ cups reduced-sugar ketchup, such as Heinz

½ cup Onion-Garlic Puree (page 213)

¼ cup Worcestershire sauce

2 tablespoons yellow mustard

¼ cup cider vinegar

1 tablespoon molasses

2 packets (7 g) Truvia

1 teaspoon garlic salt

2 tablespoons liquid smoke, such as Stubb's

1. Combine all the ingredients in a medium saucepan over medium heat. Bring to a simmer, then reduce the heat to low. Simmer, stirring occasionally, until the sauce is thick, about 30 minutes.

2. Allow the sauce to cool. Store it in a covered container in the refrigerator for up to 5 days.

NOW YOU CAN **EAT THIS!**

	Before	After
Fat	11.8 g	**0.1 g**
Calories	142	**22**

Protein: 0 g | Carbohydrates: 5 g
Cholesterol: 0 g | Fiber: 0 g
Sodium: 142 mg

ROCKIN' ASIAN STIR-FRY SAUCE

1 tablespoon toasted sesame oil

¼ cup chopped fresh ginger

6 garlic cloves, minced

½ bunch scallions (white and green parts), chopped fine

1 tablespoon cornstarch

6 tablespoons soy sauce

¾ cup low-fat, low-sodium chicken broth

3 tablespoons rice vinegar

½ cup reduced-sugar ketchup, such as Heinz

Salt and freshly ground black pepper

You can buy all-purpose Asian sauces at the grocery store, but most of them are loaded with sugar and fat. This one—with lots of ginger and garlic and just a little bit of oil—is very flavorful. **Makes 1¾ cups (28 servings)**

1. Heat a large nonstick sauté pan over high heat. When the pan is hot, add the sesame oil. Add the ginger, garlic, and scallions, and sauté, stirring often, until very fragrant, about 2 minutes.

2. Meanwhile, place the cornstarch in a medium bowl. Add the soy sauce, chicken broth, rice vinegar, and ketchup, and whisk to blend.

3. Whisk the cornstarch mixture into the sauté pan and bring the sauce to a simmer. Reduce the heat to medium and simmer, whisking constantly, until the sauce has thickened, about 2 minutes. Season with salt and pepper to taste, if desired.

4. Store the sauce in a covered container in refrigerator for up to 1 week.

NOW YOU CAN **EAT THIS!**

	Before	After
Fat	1 g	**0.5 g**
Calories	25	**12**

Protein: 0 g | Carbohydrates: 1 g
Cholesterol: 0 mg | Fiber: 0 g
Sodium: 233 mg

NOW EAT THIS! SAUCES

SWEET AND SPICY GARLIC WING SAUCE

This sauce is great on chicken wings, of course, but it's also very tasty on steak, grilled fish, and barbecued shrimp—even on cooked greens like kale and collards. It's an all-purpose sauce based on Buffalo wing sauce—with a twist. The most important twist may be that it has zero fat and only 33 calories per serving. Traditional Buffalo wing sauce is loaded with butter. **Makes 1¼ cups (10 servings)**

1. In a small saucepan over medium heat, combine the wing sauce, ketchup, garlic, orange juice concentrate, Worcestershire sauce, salt to taste, and Truvia. Bring the mixture to a simmer. Then reduce the heat to low and simmer for 15 minutes.

2. Let the sauce cool. Store it in a covered container in the refrigerator for up to 1 week.

⅓ cup Frank's RedHot Buffalo Wings Sauce

1 cup reduced-sugar ketchup, such as Heinz

8 garlic cloves, minced

2 tablespoons orange juice concentrate, thawed

2 tablespoons Worcestershire sauce

Salt

4 packets (14 g) Truvia

NOW YOU CAN **EAT THIS!**

	Before	After
Fat	4g	**1.3 g**
Calories	50	**33**

Protein: 0 g | Carbohydrates: 5 g
Cholesterol: 0 mg | Fiber: 0 g
Sodium: 276 mg

BASIC GRAVY

2 garlic cloves, minced

½ cup yellow onion, roughly chopped

½ cup carrot, roughly chopped

½ cup celery root, roughly chopped

1 large sprig fresh thyme

1½ cups nonfat, low-sodium chicken broth, plus more if needed

Salt and freshly ground black pepper

Most gravies are made from meat juices and a thickener called "roux," a 50/50 combination of pure fat—like lard or butter—and white flour. This flourless, butterless gravy can be used as a stand-alone sauce for almost any roast meat or poultry—and even some fish like cod and salmon. Play around with it: add low-fat bacon pieces, chopped olives, parsley, tarragon, basil, roasted pearl onions, diced cooked sweet potatoes, lemon zest, crushed peppercorns—whatever you can think of that fits into your caloric budget. **Makes 2½ cups (10 servings)**

1. Combine the garlic, onion, carrot, celery root, thyme sprig and chicken broth in a large saucepan over high heat. Season with salt and pepper to taste, cover, and bring to a boil. Then reduce the heat and simmer until the vegetables are tender, about 12 minutes.

2. Remove the thyme sprig. Pour the contents of the pot into a blender container. Being careful of steam buildup in the blender, blend the mixture until it is smooth, adding a little more chicken broth if necessary to achieve a gravy consistency. Serve, or store in a covered container in the refrigerator for up to 3 days.

NOW YOU CAN **EAT THIS!**

	Before	After
Fat	5.5 g	**0.1 g**
Calories	80	**12**

Protein: 1 g | Carbohydrates: 2 g
Cholesterol: 0 mg | Fiber: 0 g
Sodium: 156 mg

ONION-GARLIC PUREE

This aromatic puree is designed to be a base ingredient and is a great way to build flavor and texture without adding fat. It eliminates the need to add a lot of butter and cream to Macaroni and Cheese with a Crusty Crunch (page 174), for instance. You can stir it into just about any sauce or soup for a fat-free flavor punch. **Makes 1 cup**

1 large Vidalia onion, roughly chopped

9 garlic cloves, roughly chopped

½ cup water

Salt and freshly ground black pepper

1. Combine the onion, garlic, and water in a microwave-safe bowl. Season with salt and pepper to taste. Cover the bowl tightly with plastic wrap, and microwave on high for 10 minutes.

2. Pour the mixture into a blender and blend until it is completely smooth. Season with salt and pepper to taste, if desired. Store in a covered container in the refrigerator for up to 72 hours.

NOW YOU CAN **EAT THIS!**

	Before	After
Fat	NA	**0.3 g**
Calories	NA	**85**

Protein: 3 g | Carbohydrates: 19 g
Cholesterol: 0 mg | Fiber: 3 g
Sodium: 594 mg

"Russian Island" Dressing (top), Hollandaise Sauce (middle), and Tartar Sauce (bottom).

HOLLANDAISE SAUCE

I know, I am a fool for even trying to take on a butter sauce for this book, but I would be remiss if I didn't. In doing my research, many of you expressed your delight with this magical buttery emulsion, and I have to confess I am a fan as well. When I was a young chef, we used to have contests to see who could make the best hollandaise sauce. It's actually a lot of fun to make because the chemical reaction that takes place makes it a bit challenging. This version is virtually impossible to mess up because when you remove most of the butter, you don't have to worry about tricky emulsifications and the sauce "breaking" if the heat is too high. While it's not the butter bomb that the original is, having only one-third of the original fat and calories is worth making some adjustments for. **Makes 1¹/₃ cups (about 7 servings)**

2 tablespoons cornstarch

1 tablespoon Butter Buds Sprinkles

¼ cup plus 1 tablespoon fresh lemon juice

1 cup low-fat, low-sodium chicken broth

1 egg yolk, lightly beaten

2 tablespoons unsalted butter

Salt and freshly ground black pepper

Tabasco sauce

1. Combine the cornstarch and Butter Buds in a small saucepan. Whisk the lemon juice and chicken broth into the cornstarch mixture. Set the pan over medium-high heat and cook, whisking constantly, until the mixture boils. Then cook until thickened, about 1 minute.

2. Place the egg yolk in a small bowl. Whisk ½ cup of the hot liquid, 1 tablespoon at a time, into the egg yolk. Then whisk the warmed yolk back into the saucepan. Bring the mixture to a boil, whisking constantly. Remove the pan from the heat and whisk in the butter. Season to taste with salt, pepper, and Tabasco sauce. Serve immediately.

NOW YOU CAN **EAT THIS!**

	Before	After
Fat	13g	**3.9 g**
Calories	140	**53**

Protein: 1 g | Carbohydrates: 4 g
Cholesterol: 39 mg | Fiber: 0 g
Sodium: 219 mg

AU POIVRE SAUCE

1 tablespoon unsalted butter

2 small shallots, chopped fine (¼ cup)

2 tablespoons crushed pepper medley

3 tablespoons brandy or Cognac

½ cup low-fat, low-sodium beef broth

1 cup evaporated skim milk

1 tablespoon plus 1 teaspoon cornstarch

Salt

This rich French sauce made of pepper, Cognac, and cream is traditionally served on steak, but it's equally good on pork or salmon. Instead of cream, this version is given body and richness with cornstarch-thickened evaporated milk. **Makes 1⅓ cups**

1. Heat a large nonstick sauté pan over medium heat. When the pan is hot, add the butter. When the butter has melted, add the shallots and sauté, stirring occasionally, until they are nearly translucent, about 2 minutes.

2. Raise the heat to high, and add the pepper and brandy to the pan. Simmer the brandy for one minute. Add the broth and bring to a boil. Cook until the mixture has reduced to about ⅓ cup, about 5 minutes.

3. Meanwhile, in a small bowl, whisk the evaporated milk into the cornstarch.

4. Whisk the cornstarch mixture into the sauce. Cook, whisking constantly, until the sauce has thickened, about 2 minutes. Season with salt to taste, and serve.

NOW YOU CAN **EAT THIS!**

	Before	After
Fat	14g	**0.6 g**
Calories	152	**23**

Protein: 1 g | Carbohydrates: 2 g
Cholesterol: 2 mg | Fiber: 0 g
Sodium: 51 mg

Healthy Tips

Got (evaporated) milk? Try replacing heavy cream with evaporated skim milk in cooked foods like sauces, custards, pies, and cakes. At 25 calories per 2-tablespoon serving, compared to 40 calories for cream (and none of those coming from fat), you can have your custard and eat it, too.

TARTAR SAUCE

There are many ways to flavor tartar sauce. I like cornichons, capers, onions, and Worcestershire sauce (it's a great flavoring with little caloric significance). There are also many uses for tartar sauce—it's not just for fried fish. Try it with grilled steak or shrimp, or as a spread on a sandwich. **Makes 1¼ cups (10 servings)** (see photograph on page 214)

1 cup Rocco's Magnificent Mayonnaise (page 200) or store-bought reduced-fat mayonnaise, such as Hellmann's Low-Fat Mayonnaise Dressing

Grated zest of 1 lemon

2 tablespoons fresh lemon juice

4 cornichons, chopped fine

2 tablespoons capers, chopped

1 teaspoon Worcestershire sauce

1 small red onion, chopped fine

3 tablespoons chopped fresh flat-leaf parsley

1 packet (3.5 g) Truvia

Salt and freshly ground black pepper

Pinch of cayenne pepper

1. In a large bowl, whisk together the mayonnaise, lemon zest, lemon juice, cornichons, capers, Worcestershire sauce, onions, parsley, and Truvia. Season the sauce to taste with salt, pepper, and cayenne. Cover, and chill in the refrigerator until cold, about 1 hour.

2. Store in a covered container in the refrigerator for up to 3 days.

Healthy Tips

For a quick and delicious cold low-calorie sauce for cocktail shrimp or leftover roast meats, season low-fat mayonnaise with a little curry powder.

NOW YOU CAN **EAT THIS!**

	Before	After
Fat	14.2g	**1.9 g**
Calories	142	**48**

Protein: 1 g | Carbohydrates: 7 g
Cholesterol: 5 mg | Fiber: 0 g
Sodium: 315 mg

COCKTAIL SAUCE

1 cup reduced-sugar ketchup, such as Heinz

¼ cup prepared horseradish

1 tablespoon fresh lemon juice

1 teaspoon Worcestershire sauce

1 teaspoon hot sauce, such as Frank's RedHot Original

This slightly spicy horseradish-tomato concoction makes a one-note boiled shrimp sing like a tenor. The typical ingredients are mostly healthy except for the sugar load—usually in the form of high-fructose corn syrup. This recipe calls for reduced-sugar ketchup and all the usual suspects, including prepared horseradish. Don't mess with grating fresh horseradish—believe it or not, it's not as strong as the jarred stuff. **Makes 1¼ cups (20 servings)**

Whisk all the ingredients together in a medium bowl until well combined. Cover, and chill in the refrigerator until cold, about 1 hour. Store in a covered container in the refrigerator for up to 1 week.

NOW YOU CAN EAT THIS!

	Before	After
Fat	0.3g	0 g
Calories	30	6

Protein: 0 g | Carbohydrates: 1 g
Cholesterol: 0 mg | Fiber: 0 g
Sodium: 24 mg

"These recipes are all about having your cake (and apple pie and tiramisu and cobbler and brownies) and eating it too. Who says dessert can't be healthy and taste good?"

DESSERTS

STRAWBERRY GRAHAM CRACKER TARTS

½ vanilla bean, split, seeds scraped out and reserved

2 ounces low-fat cream cheese

3 tablespoons granulated Splenda or 9 packets (31.5 g) Truvia

1¼ cups nonfat Greek yogurt

2 tablespoons pomegranate juice

4 mini graham cracker tart shells, such as Keebler

8 large fresh strawberries, sliced thin

When you think about adding flavor to foods in the most healthful way possible, you think about the most intense flavor vehicles you can find. That's why this recipe calls for vanilla bean. The tiny seeds inside pack a wallop of this most delicate and beloved taste. If you can't find good strawberries, try whole raspberries or small slices of ripe peach. **Serves 4**

1. In the bowl of an electric mixer fitted with the paddle attachment, combine the vanilla bean seeds, cream cheese, and Splenda. Beat until the mixture is slightly fluffy, about 1 minute.

2. Scrape down the sides of the bowl. Add the yogurt and pomegranate juice. Beat until the yogurt is fully incorporated, about 1 minute. Scrape down the sides of the bowl, and beat for 1 minute more.

3. Fill each tart shell with the cream cheese mixture. Arrange the strawberry slices on top. Serve immediately, or refrigerate until serving time.

NOW YOU CAN **EAT THIS!**

	Before	After
Fat	NA	**8.1 g**
Calories	NA	**207**

Protein: 9 g | Carbohydrates: 24 g
Cholesterol: 10 mg | Fiber: 1 g
Sodium: 212 mg

Healthy Tips

Try a new kind of strawberries and cream: In a small bowl, crush 2 large ripe strawberries with a fork. Then stir in 1 packet of Truvia and 2 ounces (¼ cup) of nonfat Greek yogurt. Satisfies your sweet tooth for fewer than 50 calories.

REAL CHOCOLATE MOUSSE

"To truly mousse or not to mousse?" That was the question. At first I thought I'd find a great low-fat packaged mousse mix and turn the flavors up by adding some interesting ingredients. I tried it…and decided you deserved better. This is as close as I could get to a real chocolate mousse, made with egg whites and chocolate and very little fat. **Serves 4**

1. Combine the vanilla and 1 teaspoon water in a medium bowl. Sprinkle the gelatin on top, and set it aside for 3 to 5 minutes to allow the gelatin to bloom.

2. Bring a medium pot of water to a simmer. Meanwhile, in a metal bowl, whisk together the egg substitute, unsweetened chocolate, agave nectar, salt, and espresso powder. Place the bowl over the simmering water and whisk until the chocolate is fully melted and the mixture is hot and thickened. Do not allow the egg substitute to fully cook. (You can also do this in a double boiler.) Whisk the hot chocolate mixture into the bloomed gelatin until the gelatin is melted and fully incorporated. Allow the chocolate mixture to cool to room temperature, stirring occasionally. This will take only a few minutes.

3. When the chocolate mixture has cooled, place the egg whites in the bowl of an electric mixer fitted with the whip attachment, and begin to beat them on medium speed. When they begin to foam, add the cream of tartar. When very soft peaks begin to form, gradually add the Splenda. Whip the whites until they form medium peaks. They should look somewhat creamy and should not be stiff or dry.

4. Fold one-third of the egg whites into the chocolate mixture to lighten it. Then, in two increments, fold the chocolate mixture into the whites until it is just incorporated. Spoon the mousse into 4 dessert dishes, and refrigerate for 1 hour or up to 5 hours.

5. Sprinkle the chocolate chips, raspberries, and sliced strawberries on top, and serve.

1 teaspoon vanilla extract

½ teaspoon powdered gelatin

⅓ cup egg substitute

1½ ounces unsweetened chocolate, chopped fine

1 tablespoon light agave nectar

Pinch of salt

2 tablespoons instant espresso powder

4 large egg whites, at room temperature

¼ teaspoon cream of tartar

¼ cup granulated Splenda

2 tablespoons semisweet chocolate chips

½ cup fresh raspberries

½ cup sliced fresh strawberries

NOW YOU CAN **EAT THIS!**

	Before	After
Fat	32.3g	**7.2 g**
Calories	455	**145**

Protein: 8 g | Carbohydrates: 17 g
Cholesterol: 0 mg | Fiber: 3 g
Sodium: 168 mg

CLASSIC TIRAMISÙ

20 ounces nonfat Greek yogurt

3 ounces mascarpone cheese

2 tablespoons dry Marsala wine

½ cup plus 2 tablespoons granulated Splenda

20 ladyfingers

1⅓ cups brewed cold espresso

2 tablespoons unsweetened cocoa powder

Tiramisù is a high-calorie dessert if there ever was one. I started the makeover process thinking the lighter version should include from-scratch sugar-free ladyfingers—homemade génoise piped in perfect finger shapes and baked. Then I got my head screwed on straight and realized that no one would make this dessert if it meant making your own génoise. The fat-laden original was transformed into something even an Italian grandma would love. **Serves 12**

1. In the bowl of a standing mixer fitted with the whip attachment, combine the yogurt, mascarpone, Marsala, and Splenda. Whip the ingredients on high speed for 1 minute. Scrape down the sides of the bowl and continue to whip until smooth, about another 30 seconds.

2. Arrange 10 of the ladyfingers in the bottom of an 8×8-inch glass dish. Using a pastry brush, brush the ladyfingers with half of the espresso. Spoon half of the mascarpone mixture over the ladyfingers, and using an offset spatula, spread the mixture evenly to cover the ladyfingers.

3. Top the mascarpone layer with the remaining 10 ladyfingers, and repeat the soaking process with the remaining espresso. Spread the remaining mascarpone mixture over the ladyfingers. Cover the tiramisù lightly with plastic wrap, and chill it in the refrigerator for at least 1 hour or up to 24 hours.

4. Use a sieve to sprinkle the cocoa powder evenly over the top, and serve.

NOW YOU CAN EAT THIS!

	Before	After
Fat	32g	**4.2g**
Calories	510	**120**

Protein: 7 g | Carbohydrates: 15 g
Cholesterol: 48 mg | Fiber: 0 g
Sodium: 84 mg

Healthy Tips

For more pound-for-pound chocolate flavor and an easy 35 percent reduction in fat calories in your chocolate dessert recipes, replace regular unsweetened cocoa powder (12 percent fat) with defatted unsweetened cocoa powder (.05 percent fat).

APPLE PIE

filling

1½ teaspoons ground cinnamon

½ teaspoon salt

1 teaspoon cornstarch

6 packets (21 g) Truvia

10 medium to large Granny Smith apples, peeled, cored, and cut into ⅓-inch-thick slices

topping

¼ cup plus 2 tablespoons old-fashioned rolled oats

¾ cup granulated Splenda

½ cup whole-wheat pastry flour, such as Whole Foods' 365 Everyday Value

½ teaspoon salt

1 teaspoon ground cinnamon

4 tablespoons very cold un-salted butter, cut into small chunks

¼ cup chopped pecans

½ large egg white

This country was built on apple pie with a very flaky crust, thanks to an abundance of lard or vegetable shortening. Instead of an overly caloric full-blown crust, this lightened-up pie has a crumbly Brown Betty–type topping. When you pulse the topping mixture, don't over-mix or it will be tough—not melt-in-your-mouth tender. If you must serve ice cream with this pie, look for a low-cal alternative. The usual scoop of "à la mode" adds 250 to 350 calories. **Serves 12**

1. Preheat the oven to 400°F.

2. To make the filling: In a large bowl, mix together the cinna-mon, salt, cornstarch, and Truvia. Add the apples and toss with the cinnamon mixture. Transfer the apples to a 9-inch glass bak-ing dish, mounding them high.

3. To make the topping: Combine the oats, Splenda, flour, salt, and cinnamon in the bowl of a food processor, and pulse just to combine. Add the butter and pecans, and pulse a few times to make a crumbly mixture. Add the egg white and pulse a few times, until small clumps of crumble start to form. Scatter the crumble mixture over the apples, covering as much surface area as possible.

4. Cover the pie with aluminum foil and bake for 1 hour. Raise the oven temperature to 425°F, remove the foil, and continue to bake until the apples are tender and the crumble topping is golden brown, about 15 minutes. Allow the pie to rest for 5 min-utes and serve warm.

NOW YOU CAN **EAT THIS!**

	Before	After
Fat	53g	**5.9 g**
Calories	1,203	**132**

Protein: 2 g | Carbohydrates: 22 g
Cholesterol: 10 mg | Fiber: 3 g
Sodium: 197 mg

CRÈME BRÛLÉE

Even though there is no sugar in the custard part of the recipe, I did decide—after experimenting with every sugar substitute out there—that it would be okay to use unrefined Demerara sugar for the brûlée part of this dessert. Considering that the fat grams are down to less than 3 from 50, I gave myself a pass. **Serves 4**

1 packet gelatin

1⅔ cups 2% milk

2 tablespoons plus 1 teaspoon cornstarch

9 packets (31.5 g) Truvia

¼ vanilla bean, seeds scraped out and reserved

1 large pinch salt

2 tablespoons Greek yogurt

2 tablespoons Turbinado sugar, such as Sugar in the Raw

1. Empty the gelatin packet into a medium bowl. Pour 2 tablespoons of the milk over the gelatin, and set it aside to soften for at least 3 minutes.

2. In a small saucepan, whisk the remaining milk into the cornstarch. Whisk in the Truvia, vanilla bean and seeds, and salt. Bring the milk mixture to a boil over high heat, whisking constantly. When it boils, reduce the heat to low and continue to cook until it has thickened, about 30 seconds. Remove and discard the vanilla bean. Whisk about ⅓ cup of the thickened milk mixture into the softened gelatin to melt it. Then whisk in the remaining milk mixture. Whisk the yogurt into the gelatin-milk mixture.

3. Divide the mixture among four 3½×2-inch ramekins. Chill covered in refrigerator until completely set and cold, about 2 hours.

4. Sprinkle each crème brûlée with ½ tablespoon of the Demerara sugar. Using a kitchen blowtorch, burn the sugar until it is a deeply caramelized golden brown. Serve immediately.

Healthy Tips

If you are committed to making this wonderful dessert, you must also commit to using a kitchen blowtorch. There simply is no alternative for achieving that crunchy caramelized topping that the intense heat delivers. You can buy a more expensive version at gourmet cookware stores, or pick one up for $25 (including the replaceable propane tank) at your local hardware store. Plus, you never know when you might have to do some plumbing!

NOW YOU CAN **EAT THIS!**

	Before	After
Fat	50.2g	**2.7 g**
Calories	562	**116**

Protein: 5 g | Carbohydrates: 18 g
Cholesterol: 10 mg | Fiber: 0 g
Sodium: 123 mg

PEACH AND BLUEBERRY COBBLER WITH GINGER AND CINNAMON

This is a gorgeous dessert and naturally low in calories, as long as you don't add a ton of sugar and don't serve it with whipped cream. It just doesn't need it. In the heat of the oven, as they steam under the topping, the peaches and blueberries meld into a magical, flavorful filling that needs little help from sugar or fat. The spices are really all the fruit requires. **Serves 8**

1. Preheat the oven to 425°F. Spray a 7×11-inch glass baking dish with cooking spray, and set it aside.

2. In a medium bowl, mix together the peaches, blueberries, the ¼ cup Splenda, and the 1 tablespoon baking mix. Pour the fruit mixture into the prepared baking dish.

3. In a medium bowl, combine the remaining 2 tablespoons Splenda, the remaining ¾ cup Bisquick, and the ginger, cinnamon, and milk. Stir until the mixture forms a soft dough. Drop spoonfuls of the dough evenly over the fruit mixture. Sprinkle the sugar over the dough.

4. Bake the cobbler until the fruit is tender and the biscuit topping is golden brown, about 30 minutes. Let it rest for 5 minutes before serving.

Nonstick cooking spray

4 ripe peaches, peeled, pitted, and sliced

1 cup fresh blueberries

¼ cup plus 2 tablespoons granulated Splenda

¾ cup plus 1 tablespoon Bisquick Heart Smart baking mix

1 teaspoon ground ginger

¼ teaspoon ground cinnamon

⅓ cup skim milk

2 tablespoons Turbinado sugar, such as Sugar In The Raw

NOW YOU CAN **EAT THIS!**

	Before	After
Fat	33g	**1 g**
Calories	681	**96**

Protein: 2 g | Carbohydrates: 22 g
Cholesterol: 0 mg | Fiber: 2 g
Sodium: 158 mg

RICE PUDDING

2 cups water

Pinch of salt

5 packets (17.5 g) Truvia

¼ vanilla bean, split, seeds scraped out and reserved

½ cup long-grain brown rice

¼ cup raisins

½ cup Greek yogurt

¼ cup skim milk

¼ teaspoon ground cinnamon

Traditional rice pudding contains cream, eggs, and sugar. You'll find none of that here. You *will* find healthful whole-grain brown rice, raisins, creamy Greek yogurt, and lovely flavor from real vanilla bean and cinnamon. Eat any leftovers for breakfast. **Serves 4**

1. Combine the water, salt, Truvia, vanilla bean and seeds, and rice in a medium saucepan, and bring to a simmer. Cover, and reduce the heat to low. Simmer gently for 55 minutes.

2. Stir in the raisins and continue to cook until almost all the liquid has been absorbed and the rice is tender, about 15 minutes.

3. Allow the rice mixture to cool for about 10 minutes. Then transfer it to a medium bowl, discarding the vanilla pod. Stir in the yogurt, milk, and cinnamon. Adjust the consistency with a little water, if desired. Serve warm.

NOW YOU CAN **EAT THIS!**

	Before	After
Fat	47.6 g	**3.5 g**
Calories	745	**156**

Protein: 4 g | Carbohydrates: 28 g
Cholesterol: 8 mg | Fiber: 1 g
Sodium: 65 mg

TRIPLE CHOCOLATE CHOCOLATE CHIP COOKIES

This recipe took almost three weeks of trial and error before I perfected it. But the fantastic result was well worth the aggravation! With three kinds of chocolate for flavor—cocoa powder, cacao nibs, and chocolate chips—you won't miss the fat and sugar in the standard version of this most beloved cookie. Pour a glass of (skim) milk and get happy. **Makes 20 cookies**

Nonstick cooking spray

½ teaspoon vanilla extract

⅓ cup unsweetened cocoa powder, sifted

1 cup canned white cannellini beans, rinsed and drained

2 tablespoons light agave syrup

3 large egg whites

1½ cups granulated Splenda

¼ cup dark chocolate-covered cacao nibs

¼ cup mini chocolate chips

1. Preheat the oven to 375°F. Line 2 baking sheets with parchment paper and spray lightly with cooking spray. Set aside.

2. In the bowl of a food processor, combine vanilla, cocoa, cannellini beans, and the agave syrup, and blend the mixture until smooth, about 3 minutes, scraping down the side of the bowl halfway through blending.

3. In the bowl of a mixer fitted with a whip attachment, beat the egg whites until they form soft peaks. Gradually beat in the Splenda. Continue to beat the whites until they are creamy and nearly stiff. Add one-third of the egg-white mixture to the cocoa-bean mixture in the food processor. Blend to combine, about 30 seconds. In 2 batches, fold the lightened cocoa mixture into the egg whites until they are almost fully combined. Add cacao nibs to the batter. Fold batter until cacao nibs are evenly dispersed and cocoa mixture is completely incorporated.

4. Drop mounded spoonfuls of batter onto the prepared sheets. Spread batter out to form cookies about 2½ inches in diameter. Sprinkle the chocolate chips on top of the cookies.

5. Bake for 20 minutes, rotating the pans one turn halfway through baking. Using a metal spatula, transfer cookies to wire racks to cool.

NOW YOU CAN **EAT THIS!**

	Before	After
Fat	10g	**1.4 g**
Calories	210	**45**

Protein: 2 g | Carbohydrates: 9 g
Cholesterol: 0 mg | Fiber: 2 g
Sodium: 32 mg

BROWNIES

Yes, you are reading the ingredients list correctly: there are black beans in these brownies. You really have to taste the brownies to believe them. The beans add moisture and texture—not to mention fiber and protein. These brownies have such a great fudgy texture because the cocoa powder, and just a little espresso powder, are the only dry ingredients (besides a bit of Truvia). For an extra jolt of chocolate flavor and about 15 more calories, stir ¼ cup dark chocolate–covered cacao nibs (such as Kopali Organics) into the batter just before pouring it into the pan. These brownies are even better the next day.

Serves 12

1. Preheat the oven to 350°F. Spray an 8×8-inch glass baking dish with cooking spray.

2. Combine the beans, cocoa powder, espresso powder, and egg substitute in the bowl of a food processor. Process until the mixture is smooth, about 2 minutes, scraping down the bowl halfway through.

3. Add the chocolate syrup, sour cream, butter, Truvia, and vanilla. Process until all of the ingredients are combined, about 1 minute.

4. Pour the batter into the prepared baking dish, and smooth the top with a spatula. Bake for 28 to 30 minutes, turning the dish halfway through the baking time. A toothpick inserted in the center will come out with soft batter clinging to it.

5. Let the brownies cool completely in the baking dish on a wire rack. Then cut into 12 squares and serve. Refrigerate any leftovers.

Nonstick cooking spray

1½ cups canned black beans, rinsed and drained

½ cup unsweetened cocoa powder

1 tablespoon espresso powder

¾ cup egg substitute

2 tablespoons low-calorie sugar-free chocolate syrup, such as Walden Farms

2 tablespoons reduced-fat sour cream, such as Breakstone's

1 tablespoon unsalted butter, melted

24 packets (84 g) Truvia or 8 tablespoons granulated Splenda

1 teaspoon vanilla extract

NOW YOU CAN **EAT THIS!**

	Before	After
Fat	70g	**1.6 g**
Calories	1,500	**53**

Protein: 4 g | Carbohydrates: 8 g
Cholesterol: 4 mg | Fiber: 3 g
Sodium: 94 mg

BERRY YUMMY FROZEN YOGURT POPS

This recipe was created for my friend Bill, who told me he couldn't get his daughter to eat fruit. I asked him what her favorite food was and the response was "ice cream." (Well, what would *you* say?) These pops are mostly fruit, with just a little bit of "ice cream" made from low-fat Greek yogurt and sugar substitute. But when the pureed fruit was mixed with it, she couldn't tell the difference. At just about 60 calories a pop, you can eat these all summer long. **Serves 8**

¾ cup fresh raspberries

¾ cup fresh blueberries

¾ cup fresh strawberries

⅓ cup granulated Splenda

Two 7-ounce containers 5% Greek yogurt

Pinch of salt

1. Combine all the ingredients in a blender and puree until the mixture is smooth. Pour the mixture into 8 freezer pop molds. Freeze for at least 4 hours and up to 2 days.

2. Run the freezer pop molds under warm water, if necessary, to unmold them.

Healthy Tips

Try a new topping on your toast: sugar-free jams, jellies, and marmalades taste as good as the original versions and have a fraction of the calories. One tablespoon of sugar-free spread contains 10 calories, compared to 49 in the sugary stuff.

NOW YOU CAN **EAT THIS!**

	Before	After
Fat	9 g	**2.8 g**
Calories	194	**61**

Protein: 4 g | Carbohydrates: 7 g
Cholesterol: 7 mg | Fiber: 1 g
Sodium: 60 mg

CHOCOLATE FROZEN YOGURT

2½ ounces high-quality 99% unsweetened chocolate, such as Scharffen Berger, chopped

6 tablespoons agave nectar

1½ cups skim milk

Pinch of salt

Two 7-ounce containers 2% Greek yogurt

If you're going to take the time to churn your own ice cream, I think it should be chocolate, don't you? This is sweetened with agave nectar instead of artificial sweetener because the nectar gives the finished stuff real unctuousness and body—almost like the real thing. Serves 4

1. In a small saucepan, bring the chocolate, agave nectar, milk, and salt to a simmer over medium heat. Remove the pan from the heat and whisk until smooth. Whisk ½ cup of the yogurt into the warm chocolate mixture. Then add the remaining yogurt and whisk until the mixture is smooth.

2. Freeze the yogurt mixture in an ice cream maker according to the manufacturer's directions. Serve immediately, or transfer to a tightly sealed container and freeze up to 2 days.

NOW YOU CAN EAT THIS!

	Before	After
Fat	32 g	11.4 g
Calories	521	276

Protein: 14 g | Carbohydrates: 38 g
Cholesterol: 8 mg | Fiber: 3 g
Sodium: 102 mg

MINT CHOCOLATE CHIP FROZEN YOGURT

Time to go through the impulse purchases you're storing in the attic or basement and dig out that old-fashioned ice cream maker you thought you couldn't live without. Here's a very good reason to un-pack it. **Serves 4**

1. In a large bowl, sprinkle the gelatin over ½ cup of the milk. In a small saucepan, combine the remaining ¼ cup milk with the Splenda, and bring to a boil over high heat. Pour the hot mixture into the bowl, and whisk until the gelatin has dissolved.

2. Whisk the yogurt into the gelatin mixture. Whisk in the peppermint extract and a drop or two of the green food coloring, enough to achieve the desired color.

3. Freeze the mixture in an ice cream maker according to the manufacturer's instructions. When the mixture is nearly frozen but still slightly soft, add or stir in the chopped chocolate. Serve immediately, or transfer the yogurt to a sealed container and freeze up to 2 days.

4 tablespoons powdered gelatin

¾ cup skim milk

1 cup granulated Splenda

One 17.6-ounce container nonfat Greek yogurt

½ teaspoon organic peppermint extract

Green food coloring

1 ounce high-quality 99% unsweetened chocolate, such as Scharffen Berger, chopped fine

NOW YOU CAN **EAT THIS!**

	Before	After
Fat	25 g	**3.8 g**
Calories	315	**144**

Protein: 19 g | Carbohydrates: 16 g
Cholesterol: 1 mg | Fiber: 1 g
Sodium: 80 mg

index

turkey, 127–34
  Bolognese with noodles, 133
  enchiladas, cheesy, with
    tomatillo salsa and cilantro,
    128
  grilled, kebabs à la king,
    131
  grilled, Salisbury steaks with
    tomatoes and provolone sauce,
    134
  loaded nachos with black beans,
    salsa and, 25
  in Mama-approved spaghetti and
    meatballs, 278

smoked, Reuben, 75
in super-light Mexican chili con
  carne with beans, 127
tacos with tomatillo salsa,
  132

vegetable:
  lasagna, zucchini and eggplant,
    171
  see also specific vegetables
vinaigrette, not so basic, 204

walnuts, crushed, beet and blue
  cheese salad with, 52

wasabi, seared tuna with green
  beans, lemon and, 93
whole-wheat pasta, xxi

yogurt, frozen:
  chocolate, 238
    mint chocolate chip, 239
    pops, berry yummy, 237
yogurt, Greek, xix
    tahini dressing, broccoli falafel
    salad with, 6

zucchini and eggplant vegetable
  lasagna, 171

about the author

ROCCO DISPIRITO entered the Culinary Institute of America at the age of sixteen, and at eighteen began working for legendary chefs worldwide. After graduating from Boston University with a degree in business, he began working for such renowned New York chefs as Gray Kunz. In 1995 Rocco opened Dava and quickly earned two stars from Ruth Reichl at *The New York Times*. At thirty-one, Rocco opened Union Pacific in New York City and received three stars from *The New York Times*.

Hailed as one of *Food and Wine* magazine's Best New Chefs, DiSpirito is the first chef to grace the cover of *Gourmet* magazine as America's Most Exciting Young Chef, and was voted their Leading Chef of His Generation. Referred to as America's original "Rockstar Chef," Rocco has been featured in *Harper's Bazaar, Cosmopolitan, W, The New York Times, Details, House Beautiful, Us, OK!,* and *People,* including the Sexiest Man Alive issue.

DiSpirito received the James Beard Award for his first cookbook, *Flavor.* He went on to author *Rocco's Italian-American* (2004), *Rocco's Five Minute Flavor* (2005), *Rocco's Real-Life Recipes* (2007), and *Rocco Gets Real* (2009).

DiSpirito also starred in the Food Network series *Melting Pot,* the NBC hit reality series *The Restaurant,* and the A&E series *Rocco Gets Real.* He is a content partner on *Rachael Ray,* and a frequent guest on *Good Morning America* and *Top Chef.* He has appeared on *The Oprah Winfrey Show, The Ellen DeGeneres Show, Chelsea Lately, The Late Show with David Letterman, The Tonight Show with Jay Leno, Jimmy Kimmel Live,* and NBC's *The Biggest Loser,* and was the first chef to compete on the ABC megahit *Dancing with the Stars.*

In 2006 DiSpirito began his quest toward a more active and healthy life, competing in triathlons, including an Ironman 70.3. In November 2009 he was the spokesperson for and completed the Ironman in Clearwater, Florida, setting a personal-best time.

Rocco lives in New York City and appreciates all that cooking has brought to him.